ultimate
Scrapbook Style

ultimate
Scrapbook Style

A creative technique and design guide for victorian, retro, and contemporary pages

Trice Boerens

GLOUCESTER MASSACHUSETTS

QUARRY BOOKS

First published in the United States of America by
Quarry Books, a member of
Quayside Publishing Group
33 Commercial Street
Gloucester, Massachusetts 01930-5089
Telephone: (978) 282-9590
Fax: (978) 283-2742
www.rockpub.com

Library of Congress Cataloging-in-Publication Data
Boerens, Trice.
    Ultimate scrapbook style: a creative technique and design guide for Victorian, retro, and contemporary pages / Trice Boerens.
        p.   cm.
    ISBN 1-59253-256-X (pbk.)
    1. Photograph albums. 2. Photographs—Conservation and restoration.
3. Scrapbooks. I. Title.
TR465.B688 2006
745.593—dc22   2005033057
                                                              CIP

ISBN 1-59253-256-X

10 9 8 7 6 5 4 3 2 1

Design: James Casey Design
Layout and Production: *tabula rasa* graphic design
Templates: Cherie Hanson
Cover Image and Photography: Kevin Dilley/Klik Photo

Printed in Singapore

This book is dedicated to curious people.

"We keep moving forward, opening new doors, and doing new things, because we're curious and curiosity keeps leading us down new paths." —Walt Disney

flowers

love

laughter

invitations

life

family

memories

CONTENTS

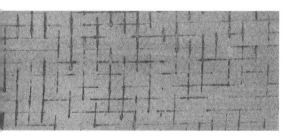

INTRODUCTION

AFTER HANGING OUT in the scrapbook world for the past several years, it is hard not to notice that most instructional materials are technique driven. Book and magazine publishers have done a superb job of introducing new and intriguing ways of manipulating paper and embellishing it with anything that fits on a page—and a few things that don't. The presentation and instruction are so well done that I often find myself leafing through a magazine at a checkout aisle, seeing something exciting, and racing home to try it myself.

The emphasis of this book is to present a variety of design styles for your pages. When designing with a specific style in mind, your finished projects will have a uniform look and a personality that can't be beat. The ideas collected here will help you do some creative time traveling. For example, if you happen upon a photo of your mother wearing white lipstick and even whiter go-go boots, you can scan the '60s section for techniques and layout ideas that will enhance your photo and reflect the styles of the day. Or you may want to show off a contemporary wedding photo on an overly ornate Victorian page. In addition to stylish layout, you'll learn a range of craft techniques, many of which have roots in historic periods. With forty techniques included, there is some overlap between the style periods. For example, a

'60s page with an emphasis on embroidery also has pressed flowers added to it. However, the Pressed Flowers technique is found in the Victorian section.

Beginning with the Victorian Style section, you will recognize a style that began more than one hundred years ago and is still going strong. It lends itself to event pages of weddings, births, and parties, and of course to honoring beloved ancestors.

There is nothing more popular today than the retro styles of yesterday. The hottest-selling clothing, home decor, and furniture looks as if it came straight out of the pages of '60s and '70s consumer catalogs. And flash back to the '50s section, which captures the sweetness and sentimentality of that era.

The Contemporary Style section encompasses many intriguing paper fashions, since today's tastes are far reaching. The techniques with which you already may be familiar are redefined and presented in fresh ways. New techniques are also introduced to keep you ahead of the curve.

Working for many years as a needlework designer, I was always amazed at the stunning pieces produced by needle artists. Most impressive is the idea that everything began with one needle and a single strand of thread. The same is true for paper crafting. It all starts with a flat piece of paper. So sit down with a fresh sheet and get started.

BASICS

MATERIALS

Adhesives

Many adhesives are available for assembling pages, but it is important to use glues that will not discolor the paper or cause it to become brittle or to disintegrate. Look for products that are archival quality. This means that over time, they will not damage the paper or the photos.

Archival-quality adhesive spray can be used when attaching paper to paper. It is convenient to use and can be applied evenly to the wrong side of the paper. Be sure to protect working surfaces with newspaper before spraying the adhesive because the spray covers a wide area. Specially formulated **glue dots** also work well when sticking paper to paper. Glue dots are dry adhesive circles that are packaged on strips of paper tape. Apply by pressing the wrong side of the paper shape on a dot, peeling both from the paper strip, and attaching the shape to the page.

Double-sided adhesive sheets are another good option for paper-to-paper adhesion, and for plastic-to-paper adhesion. They are used to adhere most nonpaper materials, including polyester film, fabric, and beads, because the adhesive film grips tightly and can be cut to any shape or configuration. This product is referred to in the text as double-sided adhesive, and brand names include Peel-N-Stick and Terrifically Tacky Tape and Adhesive. Don't confuse it with cellophane tape that is sticky on both sides—this tape is too lightweight for these applications. (Note: Be sure to use scissors with nonstick blades when working with double-sided adhesive sheets.)

Paper

The paper requirements are listed as 12" x 12" (30.5 x 30.5 cm) sheets or as solid-colored or print papers. The papers with no size designation can vary from small scraps to 8½" x 11" (21.6 x 27.5 cm) sheets. Use the photo model as a reference and, if you wish, you may substitute papers with those that you may already have on hand.

TOOLS AND TECHNIQUES

Tips on Cutting

Paper and vellum shapes can be cut with scissors or with a craft knife. To sharpen dull scissors, cut through fine sandpaper several times. When using a craft knife, take care to change the blade regularly. Trimming paper quickly dulls metal blades, and cutting with a dull blade will give your paper a ragged edge. To protect your work surface when using a craft knife, use a self-healing cutting mat. Ideally, choose one with preprinted grid lines to use as guides. The lines allow you to cut uniform shapes and corners that are at right angles.

Cellophane, polyester film, and laminating plastic can also be cut with scissors or a craft knife. To cut straight lines, work over a cutting mat, and use a metal-edge ruler as a cutting guide for the craft knife, carefully running the blade along the edge. Polyester film and laminating plastic are thicker than cellophane and may require two or three passes with the knife to cut.

Fabrics should be cut with sharp scissors that are dedicated to fabric only. When making paper projects that have fabric or ribbon components, keep two pairs of scissors on hand. Use the paper scissors for paper and plastic, and the fabric scissors for fabric and ribbon only. Cutting paper with your fabric scissors will dull the blades, and when dull, they will chew up the fabric rather than cut it cleanly.

Shrink plastic can be cut with scissors or a craft knife. However, cutting curves and deep recesses can be tricky because shrink plastic is brittle. When using scissors, cut in toward the recesses from both directions to avoid cracking or breaking any appendages.

Cut metal screen with scissors or with a craft knife.

Some General Construction Tips

• Some elements are attached to the page with the edges overlapping. After securing all the paper or plastic elements to the page, trim the overlapping edges with a ruler, a craft knife, and cutting mat. Trim any overlapping fabric layers with sharp scissors.

• When it is necessary to mark the paper background for placement, lightly mark selected points with a pencil. After the page has been completed, erase them with a kneaded rubber eraser. Kneaded rubber erasers are available at art supply stores and will remove marks without damaging the paper or leaving eraser dust. Keep one on hand to rub over scuff marks or other inadvertent marks that appear on your pages.

• When hand stitching paper to paper, or fabric to paper, pierce the selected insertion points on the front of the paper before stitching. When stitching from the back to the front, you will know where to insert the needle, instead of having to guess. Stitch up and down through the pierced holes and tape the thread ends to the back of the paper.

Making Templates

To make the templates for the design shapes, layer tracing paper over the chosen shape, trace its outline, and cut along the marked lines. For paper pieces, turn over the template and trace around the outside edge. Then cut along the marked line. For cellophane, polyester film, shrink plastic, or screen shapes, tape the shapes to the material with cellophane tape, and cut along the outside edge.

Cutting Templates for Paper Piecing

Paper piecing requires transferring the individual template shapes to the colored or print papers, cutting out the shapes, and then assembling them on the page. Cut accurately to avoid gaps between the shapes, or overlap them when assembling to create a clean design. To overlap, determine the layering sequence before cutting, and cut the shapes from bottom layers slightly beyond the marked lines. Layer according to size, with the smaller shapes on top.

"Each day comes bearing its own gifts. Untie the ribbons."
—Ruth Ann Schabacker

Amy & Brody

May Thirteenth, Two thousand and five

Their parents

Brent and Holli Speechly

and

Dave and Julie Call

request the pleasure of your company

at a garden reception held in

their honor from 5:30 – 7:30 that evening

VICTORIAN STYLE

VELVET CURTAINS trimmed with tassels, tufted fainting couches, and wallpapers of bursting cabbage roses all bring to mind the romance of the Victorians. From 1837 to 1901, Queen Victoria sat on the throne of England. During this time, a design style characterized by a lush and cluttered look was fashionable in most of the Western world. The motto of the day was "the more the better." More texture, more shine, more ruffles, more prints, and on and on it went. While advances were taking place in science and technology, decorators looked to the past for inspiration, borrowing acanthus leaves from the Greeks and scrollwork from the French. They mixed in their own favorite themes of flowers, animals, and mythical creatures, and they came up with a sentimental style that continues to be popular today.

In the first half of the 1800s, fabrics were dyed as they had been for centuries, with subtle vegetable dyes. Once synthetic, or aniline, dyes were introduced, fabric colors became bright and intense. The colors were applied to everything from silk to velvet and the combinations were enthusiastic rather than discreet.

A version of the contemporary scrapbook, known as the scrap album, became wildly popular during this era. A large, bound book with an embossed leather cover, it was a glorified diary that contained personal observations, pithy sayings, and even exotic recipes. This possession became a unique showpiece and was important enough to be placed next to the family Bible in the drawing room. For illustrations, it contained what was known as ephemera, defined as transient but decorative bits and pieces of everyday life. Leaflets, handbills, tickets, playbills, labels, and advertising inserts were used to adorn the pages of Victorian scrap albums.

Pressed flowers, faux finishes, and carved hardwoods were good examples of Victorian handiwork along with gold and silver leaf surface decoration and all manner of sewing techniques: crazy quilting, ruching, beading, folding, and fringe making.

You may live in a house that is ornate enough to make the Victorians blush. But even if your interiors are clean and spare, odds are you have a crazy-quilt tablecloth or a fringed throw pillow that were fashioned in this nostalgic style. Display Victorian sensibilities on your scrapbook pages by using robust color palettes, incorporating fanciful accents and trims, and layering layout pages with abundance. The next page offers some Victorian visual inspiration before we begin exploring techniques.

Begin with floral or classical backgrounds and keep in mind that to the Victorians, accents were everything. Add folded satin, opulent charms, and heavy rayon fringe, and when you are done, add more. Can't-miss palettes include combinations of deeply saturated colors such as emerald green, burgundy, and bronze. Use pure hues of red and blue that have not been tinted with white or dulled with gray.

technique:
MARBLING

Victorians were enamored with faux paint finishes that allowed them to transform plaster into marble, and pine into burled wood. A marbling technique is adapted for paper by using a small sea sponge as an applicator. Additional materials required for this procedure include three or more colors of acrylic paint and a fine-tip paintbrush.

STEP 1

Dip the end of the sponge in the paint and blot on a paper towel. Daub the paint sparingly while rotating the sponge. (For a more organic pattern, use a sea sponge rather than a synthetic kitchen sponge.)

STEP 2

Apply a second color of paint over the first. For soft edges, apply the second layer before the first layer of paint has dried. For defined edges, apply the second layer after the first layer has dried.

STEP 3

Repeat Step 2 with the desired number of colors. To create "drifts" or flat areas of color, lightly rub, rather than daub, the sponge in random areas.

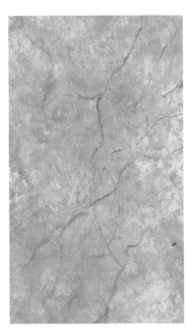

STEP 4

Use the paintbrush to make veins in the marble. Hold the tip of the brush between your thumb and forefinger and twirl it while applying the paint. The lines should be irregular in length, width, and direction.

See the projects on pages 45 and 55 that feature Marbling.

technique:
RUCHING

Ruching is a sewing technique developed by French seamstresses to make shaped ruffles or pleats. These dimensional ruffles were made from lightweight fabric and ribbon, and they decorated everything from dress cuffs to draperies. Stitched in straight, zigzag or wavy lines, the gathering threads are pulled to create lush rows, or coils. Substitute tissue paper for fabric to make accents fit for a queen.

STEP 1

Cut strips from the tissue paper. Strips can be straight, notched, or zigzagged. To make coils, cut perpendicular slits along one long side of the wide strips.

STEP 2

Layer the strips.

STEP 3

With the sewing machine, carefully stitch the gathering thread through the paper layers. For a straight ruffle, stitch a straight line down the center of the strips. For a coil, stitch a straight line along one edge of the strips. For a wavy ruffle, stitch a wavy line down the center of the zigzag strips. Secure one end of the thread with a small piece of tape, and pull the opposite end of the thread to gather.

STEP 4

Work in short increments and evenly distribute the gathers along the strips. Secure the thread ends to the back of the strip and trim.

See the projects on pages 57 and 162 that feature Ruching.

technique:
SILVER
LEAFING

A traditional art form that was taken from the church altar to the sitting room, gilded finishes of gold or silver were layered over furnishings and accessories. The metals were rolled and then pounded into thin layers, or leaves, that were 1/200,000 of an inch thick, and then painstakingly applied with glue and fine brushes. Special leafing papers of gold, silver, and copper are now available to make the gilding process easy. For a dramatic background, try covering a sheet of scrapbook paper with modern silver leaf paper. The materials needed include a sheet of paper for the background, a sheet of typing paper, rubber cement, spray adhesive, silver leaf paper, and a burnishing tool such as a pencil.

STEP 1

Cut a variety of heart shapes and sizes from the typing paper. Apply a small amount of rubber cement to the back of each shape and let dry. Arrange the shapes on the background paper and press in place. Coat the paper with spray adhesive and remove the paper shapes. Remove any residual rubber cement.

STEP 2

Place the silver leaf paper right side up on the coated paper. With the flat side of the tool, rub evenly over the entire surface.

STEP 3

Remove the silver leaf paper.

STEP 4

Use the negative spaces to show off desired decorative details.

See the projects on pages 37, 49, 59, 62, and 169 that feature Leafing.

technique:
CRAZY QUILT PIECING

The crazy quilt is the quintessential item of Victorian decor. It was originally developed to use snippets of exotic silk and satin fabrics that would collect in a woman's sewing box. Since the scraps were of all shapes and sizes, incorporating them into a single project resulted in a haphazard pattern. Today's crazy quilts can be completely random or carefully planned, with color, scale, and balance all considered to be important elements of the composition.

STEP 1

Choose lightweight coordinating fabrics. Refer to a color wheel for palette selection, and consider using monochromatic or complementary combinations. Mix together solids and patterns. Try placing some of the print fabrics wrong side up to add a halftone for blending.

STEP 2

Cut the fabrics into small pieces.

STEP 3

Coat the backs of the shapes with spray adhesive. Overlap the edges and press them in place on the page.

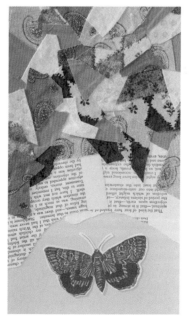

STEP 4

Trim the overlapping edges of the fabric shapes.

See the projects on pages 51 and 59 that feature Crazy Quilt Piecing.

technique:
FOLDING

Folded papers and fabrics serve as interesting accents for opulent pages. In keeping with the "more of everything" mood of the times, more dimension is a good thing. Paper is the most obvious medium to use because it is stiff and will hold a crease, but when coated with spray starch, most fabrics will work as well as paper.

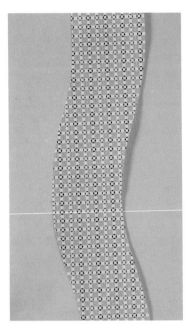

STEP 1 FOR PAPER

Cut a paper strip or paper shape. Irregular or curved shapes make a more interesting shape when folded.

STEP 2 FOR PAPER

Fold the strip. To hold the folds in place, add a contrasting strip of paper to the top, or apply a long strip of tape to the back.

STEP 1 FOR FABRIC

Cut a fabric strip or fabric shape. Irregular or curved strips make a more interesting shape when folded.

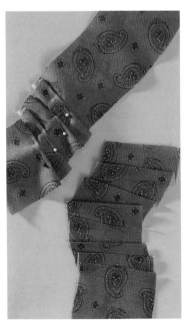

STEP 2 FOR FABRIC

Pin the folds in place and coat with spray starch. Press the fabric and remove the pins.

See the projects on pages 37, 39, 56, and 61 that feature Folding.

technique:
CARVED DETAILS

In recent years, paper crafters have made embossing a favorite technique. This involves creating raised or impressed designs in the paper surface with a metal plate and a stylus. With this idea in mind, a more dramatic raised surface is created with craft foam and wispy strips of paper. The profile and definition of the finished designs suggest an almost architectural detail. Large shapes work best so avoid floating or complex shapes. Use specialty craft foam that is porous and has adhesive on the back. Mulberry paper works best to cover the shapes because the torn edges are feathery, and it is lightweight enough to conform to the foam edges.

STEP 1
Use tracing paper to make a template.

STEP 2
Cut the shape from the foam and press it in place on the page. Tear the paper into narrow strips.

STEP 3
Coat the backs of the strips with spray adhesive and, overlapping the edges, cover the shape with the strips. It may be necessary to clip the strips to fit them around the curves and inside corners of the shape.

STEP 4
Cover the shape completely. Cover the ragged edges of the paper strips with a mat or shaped window, or leave them exposed.

See the projects on pages 43, 54, and 62 that feature Carved Details.

technique:
PRESSED FLOWERS

Nothing beats the real thing. Pressing flowers to fit in your album pages is easy to do. Make a condensed reminder of a delicate prom spray or a blooming birthday bouquet. If you are saving flowers from your garden, choose healthy blossoms with strong colors, but wait until the dew has dried before picking them. Don't forget to include leaves and ferns. Commercial flower presses are available at craft and hobby stores, but a sturdy book will do the trick.

STEP 1
Select flowers and leaves.

STEP 2
Arrange the flowers between pages of absorbent paper and place them between the pages of a book. Stack additional books on top to add weight. Wait two weeks for the flowers to dry completely.

STEP 3
Remove the pressed flowers from the book. Coat the backs of the flowers and leaves with spray adhesive.

STEP 4
Carefully press the flowers in place on the page. Alternatively, slip the flowers into a clear cellophane bag and attach the bag to the page.

See the projects on pages 42, 58, and 104 that feature Pressed Flowers.

technique:
LEOPARD PRINT STAMPS

One obsession that we share with the Victorians is the love for animal prints. Evoking exotic lands and cultures, the designs were printed on upholstery fabrics and wallpaper. Today, it is possible to sport animal print designs on your home decor, office products, tableware, and underwear. One way to add a leopard print design to all types of surfaces is with rubber stamps, so be the leader of your pack and make your own by carving rubber erasers with a craft knife. The leopard print design consists of irregular spots of brown, surrounded by stylized parentheses of black. Use the designs shown in Templates, page 180, or draw your own.

STEP 1

Draw and cut the spots and parentheses on the erasers. The templates for the spots and parentheses are on page 180.

STEP 2

With brown printing ink, stamp spots on the surface. Place them in bunches that suggest waves or drifts. Don't space them evenly or they will appear unnatural.

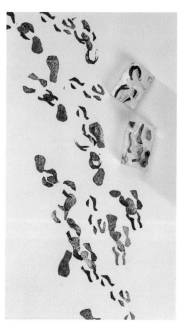

STEP 3

With the black printing ink, stamp the parentheses on the surface. Align them with the spots or stamp them in random patterns next to the spots.

STAMPED SAMPLES

Stamp plain or print papers, recycled pages from aged books, tags, or novelty papers.

See the projects on pages 39 and 40 that feature Leopard Print Stamps.

technique:
BEAD ART

Use shiny glass beads to add the shimmer and feel of fine jewelry to your paper projects. You can lightly season your page with a sprinkling of beads or add a rich flavor by covering entire areas. The texture and reflection of beads can't be beat. Three different beading techniques are represented here, so make it a point to try them all.

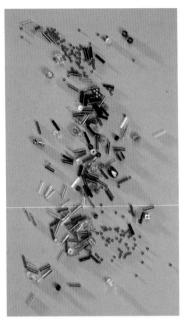

STEP 1

Choose from a wide variety of shapes and colors, including novelty shapes of flowers or bows, bugle beads (thin tubes), and seed beads (mini beads).

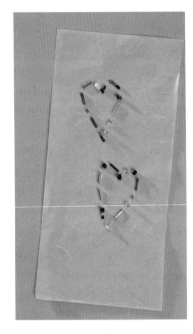

TECHNIQUE 1

Hand stitch small beads to the paper. Knot the thread end, and bring the needle from the back of the paper to the front. Tape the end to the back of the paper to secure it. Stitches should be spaced far enough apart that the needle perforations don't tear the paper. Knot the thread end, tape it to the page.

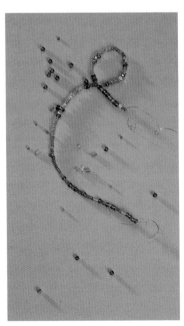

TECHNIQUE 2

Thread beads on sewing thread or fine wire. Bend and shape the strand as desired and attach it to the page with hand stitching, double-sided adhesive, or small beads of white craft glue.

TECHNIQUE 3

Cut shapes from double-sided adhesive. Peel the backing paper from the shapes and press them in place on the page. Remove the protective paper and sprinkle beads on the exposed adhesive. Remove the excess beads. Note that larger beads create more texture, and smaller beads cover more evenly.

See the projects on pages 30, 31, 34, 37, 44, 47, 54, and 60 that feature Bead Art.

technique:
QUILLED PAPER

Quilling got its name from fourteenth-century artists who carefully rolled paper strips on the ends of quills to curl them. These delicate coils were used to adorn Bible pages. Fast-forward to the nineteenth century to discover that the Victorians also used coiled paper as decoration for paper samplers and pedigree sheets. Sometimes called paper filigree, coiled papers can be pinched and shaped to resemble flowers, butterflies, and insects. It is possible to coil paper on a toothpick or a hat pin, but coils made with a quilling tool are tighter and more uniform. The process of rolling is also made easier and faster with a tool. The quilling tool is a narrow metal rod with a split tip. To coil the paper, insert the paper end in the split tip and rotate the tool in one hand while guiding the paper with the other.

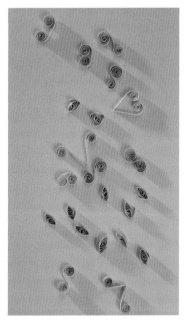

STEP 1

Choose colors from premade quilling strips, or cut your own with a metal-edge ruler and a craft knife.

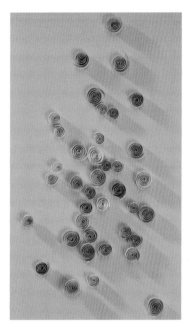

STEP 2

Cut the strips into lengths of between 2" (5.1 cm) and 6" (15.2 cm) and make coils.

STEP 3

Pinch the ends of the coils to make teardrop and elliptical shapes. Curl both ends to make "U" shapes, "V" shapes, and heart shapes.

STEP 4

Dip the shapes in white craft glue and attach them to the page.

See the projects on pages 36, 45, 49, and 52 that feature Quilled Paper.

technique:
TEA-DYED PAPER

In former times, quilters turned to natural dyes to color cotton fabrics that were available in only white or cream. Plants, including mashed beets (red), boiled onion skins (yellow), and brewed tea (brown), were all used to enhance the fibers. Tea-dyed fabric has a charming, aged appearance that can't be replicated by modern methods. To color and age white paper, dip it into brewed tea, but don't leave the paper in the tea for longer than a minute or the paper may disintegrate.

STEP 1

Brew tea using four to six tea bags for every cup of water.

STEP 2

Soak the paper in the tea for thirty seconds to a minute.

STEP 3

Remove the paper and let dry. Press the dried paper if desired.

STEP 4

Attach the paper to tags or pages with spray adhesive or glue dots.

See the projects on pages 54, 62, and 81 that feature Tea-Dyed Paper.

technique:
FRINGE

Live like a character from a fairy tale by surrounding yourself with fringe. Fringed ribbon, fringed paper, and fringed fabric all lend a light touch and mood to a page. Try all the techniques below, and then invent a few of your own.

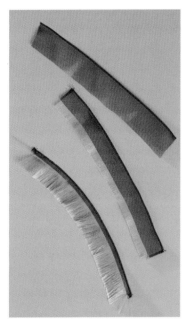

TECHNIQUE 1

Cut one side from a length of wire-edge ribbon, and pull the long threads from the cut edge to fray.

TECHNIQUE 2

Cut narrow 4" (10.2 cm) strips from selected fabric. Use them to tie evenly spaced knots on a length of narrow fringe. Trim the knot ends.

TECHNIQUE 3

Unravel the cut edges of fabrics. Rayon-blend fabrics work best.

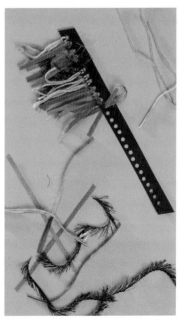

TECHNIQUE 4

Punch holes in a narrow strip of paper. Cut 4" (10.2 cm) lengths from the ribbon, floss, and decorative trim. Loop one strand through each hole and trim the ends.

See the projects on pages 38, 48, 53, and 63 that feature Fringe.

GILDED DOILY

Can't get enough glitter and glitz? Add a touch of gold to a lacy paper doily, and then use it to highlight a paper silhouette. (Refer to page 120 for Glitter.)

1. Cut two matching arch sections from a paper doily (for a total of four pieces).
2. Coat one set with adhesive spray and dip it in fine gold glitter. Let dry.
3. Attach the white arch sections to the background paper to frame a die-cut cake. Slightly offset the glitter sections, and attach them to the white sections. Add a gold pin and bits of decorative paper to finish.

MEANDERING HEART

I ❤ Victorian and this curvy free-form frame. (Refer to page 146 for Clay Art.)

1. Roll the clay to approximately ⅛" (3 mm) thick and cut from it a hollow heart shape.
2. Fold the bottom of the heart through the window to create the twisted sides.
3. Carefully reshape the heart and slightly curl the end. Bake and trim.

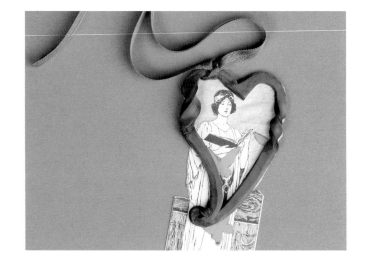

RIBBON FLUTED HEART

The texture of this heart outline brings to mind the fluted edge of a baked pie.

1. Trace a heart outline on chipboard or sturdy paper.
2. Trim around the marked lines. Cut a length of narrow silk ribbon and a length of fine silver wire, each of which is 2½ times the circumference of the heart.
3. Starting at the bottom of the heart, hold the ribbon on the heart outline and wrap the wire around both to secure. Form a small loop with the ribbon and wrap again to hold the loop in place.
4. Repeat to cover the heart outline and use it to frame a romantic message.

HAT PIN TAG

Announcing the return of the hat pin. Use this old familiar accent in a new way to secure fancy paper and tulle to a marbled tag.

1. Marble the surface of a tag.
2. Adhere additional layers of decorative paper and sequins with glue.
3. Gather a small scrap of tulle and attach to the tag with a hat pin.

COIN PURSE

Unearth an old coin purse and use it once again, this time as a snappy frame.

1. With the top edges exposed, arrange tissue paper in a coin purse.
2. Insert the bottom edge of the photo in the purse and close the clasp. Note that for a snug fit, it may be necessary to punch a small hole in the photo at the point of contact with the clasp prongs.

MINI VACATION

Scribble vacation highlights next to a mini journal spread.

1. In a paper rectangle, cut two facing windows.
2. Tape paper and a sticker to the back of the frames and attach a caption sticker to the front.
3. Crease the frame between the windows and use coordinating thread to stitch a running stitch down the center.
4. Make a paper chain to suspend the book by punching holes in narrow strips of paper.
5. Attach the strips to the corners of the book and to the backing paper with gold eyelets.

MACKINTOSH ROSES

Borrow a favorite motif from Charles Mackintosh, a Scottish architect and designer who added this simple flower to windows and furniture. (Refer to page 142 for Paper Piecing.)

1. Attach three strips of orange paper to green background paper to form a triangle.
2. Staggering the corners, attach three strips of pink paper to form another triangle over the orange triangle.
3. Center and draw a circle on the pink triangle.
4. Trim around the marked line.
5. Layer the roses on wire-veined leaves and attach them to a mini mat.

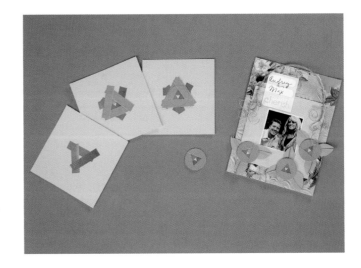

ORNAMENTS WITH BEADED CHAIN

Connect nursery ornaments with a chain made from wire and gold beads. (Refer to page 142 for Paper Piecing.)

1. Assemble paper-pieced ornaments and cut windows in each.
2. Tape stickers and pastel paper to the backs of the ornaments.
3. Thread seed beads on 32-gauge gold wire, leaving approximately 2" (5.1 cm) on each end. (Refer to page 24 for Bead Art.)
4. Thread the wire ends through small slits in the ornaments and wrap the ends around the shaped tops.
5. Tape the wire ends to the backs of the ornaments and shape the chain in a graceful coil.

YO-YO FLOWERS

Transform yo-yos into stylish flowers.

1. Trace a circle on lightweight paper.
2. Cut around the marked line and stitch a gathering thread around the outside edge of the circle.
3. Pull the thread to gather, and make a yo-yo. Flatten into a circle and secure the threads to the back of the yo-yo with tape. Trim the thread ends. Make a flower template with the same circumference, and trim the "V" shapes from the yo-yo. Do not trim around the entire outside edge of the circle or you will separate the front of the yo-yo from the back.
4. Attach the yo-yo flower to a stamped teacup and add brads and bits of ribbon.

DRAWER PULL BRACE

Sometimes all that is left of a favorite box or chest is the hardware. Add a drawer pull plate with an antique photo card and it lives on.

1. Punch pairs of small holes at the bottom of a photo card, and use fine-gauge wire to lash the hardware to the card.
2. Leaving the top ends loose, slide the bottom ends of paper ephemera under the hardware to secure.
3. Attach molded corners to the top of the card.

BLUE PLATE SPECIAL

The tag du jour is served up complete with a miniature spoon.

1. Arrange and attach paper snippets and a leather frame on a paper tag.
2. Thread the wire and ribbon through the end of the mini spoon.
3. Fan the wire and ribbon ends and tape them to the back of the paper.

SALON BEADED TAG

Great expectations mark the spot for this bejeweled tag. (Refer to page 24 for Bead Art.)

1. Arrange and attach novelty papers on the tag.
2. Draw a flower design on the paper side of a sheet of double-sided adhesive. Cut around the outside edge, remove the backing, and press in place. Cut along the marked interior lines through the protective paper. Remove a section and sprinkle the selected color on the exposed adhesive. Remove the excess beads, and repeat for the remaining colors.
3. Add a crimped paper flower and a plastic gem.

MINI PROJECTS

THEATER VALANCE

This scene-stealing treatment is deceptively easy to execute.

1. Cut paper strips and fold in half lengthwise.
2. Cut a fabric rectangle. Choose fluid, not stiff, fabric.
3. Tape the paper strips to the back of the photo card.
4. Roll the fabric lengthwise and wrap the paper strips around the fabric. Secure the ends of the strips to the front of the card with glue dots or narrow strips of double-sided adhesive.

BOX LID FRAME

A sturdy box lid becomes a shadow box frame. The most interesting are those borrowed from shaped papier-mâché boxes.

1. Trace the outline of the lid for a template and subtract the width of the lid wall.
2. Cut a shape from Fome-cor and trim the photo to match the Fome-cor shape.
3. Glue the photo to the shape.
4. Fold a long strip of fabric in half lengthwise and place it in the lid.
5. With the folded edge of the fabric exposed, push the photo inside the lid.

PAPER FRINGE

It's a snap transforming these short paper strips into festive fringe. Use lightweight, two-toned paper.

1. Cut several paper strips measuring ¾" x 2½" (1.9 x 6.4 cm). Cut waves and perpendicular slits along one long side of each strip.
2. With the wrong side up, tightly roll one end of one strip toward the center until the strip measures 1" (2.5 cm) long.
3. Attach to a basket shape with the rolled ends overlapping the flat ends. Trim to fit.

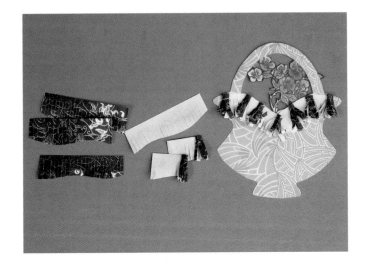

GILDED NEST

Before dreams can take flight they have to be hatched (preferably in a cozy nest made of gold).

1. Tear scraps of white tissue paper.
2. Cut a length of open weave trim.
3. Mold the trim into a nest shape. Dip the paper scraps into diluted white craft glue and mold them into egg shapes. Let dry and glue them to the bottom of the nest.

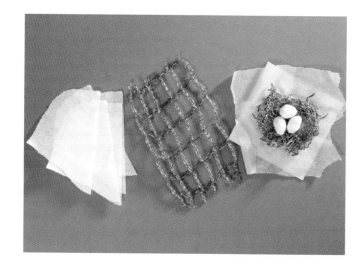

RIBBON WINDOW

Look into the past by placing an antique photo behind a curtain of folded ribbon.

1. Cut a length of wide ribbon that is slightly longer than the window.
2. Attach the ribbon to the back of the frame and cut diagonal slits from corner to corner.
3. Fold the triangular sections to the front of the frame and stitch each corner in place to secure. Add jewels or buttons if desired. Secure photo in place behind frame.

CLAY MONOGRAM

Mark your territory with a stylish monogram etched in polymer clay. (Refer to page 146 for Clay Art.)

1. Roll the clay to ¼" (6 mm) or less. Make a paper template and cut a clay shape.
2. With a sharp pencil or stylus, etch a letter in the surface. Bake the shape according to the manufacturer's directions.
3. Darken the etched line with a black colored pencil and attach the shape to the background paper.

Mini Projects

Folded Mat

With a snip here and a snip there, magically transform a boring paper mat.

1. Cut a 5" x 7" (17.8 x 12.7 cm) paper mat in half widthwise.
2. Rotate the pieces to 7" x 5" (12.7 x 17.8 cm) and fold one end of each piece at a right angle.
3. Slide together the pieces and tape the cut ends to the frame back.
4. Stitch the folded edges to the paper and cut notches in the ends.
5. Tape a vintage postcard to the back and add a paper flag.

Stork Envelope

File this birth announcement under "fetching." (Refer to page 144 for Dip-Dyed Paper.)

1. Dip the bottom half of a library envelope in green dye. Let dry.
2. Stitch a running stitch along the top edge and insert a vintage postcard.
3. If desired, cut a window in the card to reveal the artwork.
4. Add paper and clay accents.

Tissue Cake

The transitory nature of cake is represented in wafer-thin layers of hand-made paper. (Refer to page 145 for Faux Handmade Paper.)

1. With diluted white glue and white toilet tissue, make a small sheet of paper. Add bits of colored thread if desired. Let dry.
2. Cut the tiers from the paper and, with blue watercolor, paint the tops of the tiers.
3. Arrange the paper flowers, small marbled mat, bride and groom, and tiers on the paper. Attach them with glue dots or spray adhesive.
4. Cut narrow strips of double-sided adhesive and use them to attach the mini beads to the top tiers. (Refer to page 24 for Bead Art.)

ANTIQUE STITCHING

Combine two simple stitches to dress up a patchwork frame.

1. Pierce holes in the mat spaced ⅛" (3 mm) apart.
2. Stitch a running stitch through the pierced holes. On the front of the mat only, slip the needle under the running stitches, and make a wave pattern with contrasting thread.
3. Add paper and fiber accents.

APRIL FLOWERS ENVELOPE

It's raining tiny jewel-toned flowers.

1. With colored pencils, draw flowers on the etched side of shrink plastic. Note that the plastic will shrink to 50 percent of the original size.
2. Cut around the outside edge and bake according to the manufacturer's directions.
3. Fold a square of two-toned paper into a mini envelope and, with the edges exposed, insert a square of folded tissue paper.
4. Attach the flowers to the envelope with small squares of double-sided adhesive.

SUNBURST TAG

Fringed ribbon creates a second row of rays on a sunny tag.

1. Center and stamp an image on a paper disk. Punch holes around the edge.
2. Cut 5" (12.7 cm) lengths of ribbon. Fold one length in half and insert the folded end through a punched hole to form a loop. Thread the ends through the loop and pull to form a snug knot.
3. Repeat with the remaining lengths of ribbon. Trim the ribbon ends and attach the sun to a paper tag.

PEACE DOVE WITH QUILLED FLOWERS

Antique papers come to life with three-dimensional accents.

1. Glue a paper dove to backing paper.
2. Mask the center of the image and spray the edges with spray adhesive. Rub lightly with copper leaf paper. (Refer to page 18 for Silver Leafing.)
3. Cut 3" (7.6 cm) lengths of quilling paper and coil. Pinch the ends to make petal shapes and glue them to the page. (Refer to page 25 for Quilled Paper.)

QUILLED FAN

Add quilled plumage to a humble paper fan.

1. Cut a small rectangle of corrugated paper and carefully remove the flat paper backing. Cut short slits along the top edge between the ridges, and pinch the bottom of the folds together to form a fan shape. Glue the fan to the paper.
2. Fold 4½" (11.4 cm) lengths of quilling paper in half and coil the ends. Glue the coiled "V" shapes to the paper between the fan slits. (Refer to page 25 for Quilled Paper.)
3. Accent the bottom of the fan with a coiled rose and add snips of fabric and corrugated paper around the edges.

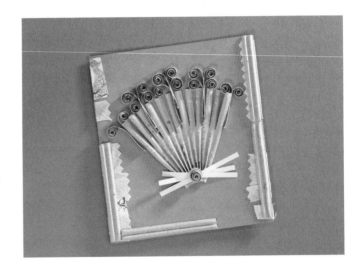

FEATHER FAN

Complement a romantic page with an easy, breezy paper fan. Print feathers combine with print paper to add the right amount of spark.

1. Cut fan sections from selected paper.
2. Attach coordinating paper to the section ends. Center and cut a small slit in each section to insert the feathers. Slide a feather in each slit and attach the end to the back with tape. Cut small holes in the bottom of each section to insert the brad.
3. Secure the brad through all layers and arrange the sections as desired.

Beaded and Pleated Tag

Colorful beads can dazzle even a black-and-white photo.

1. Trim the photo and attach it to the tag.
2. Cut a border from a sheet of double-sided adhesive. Remove the backing and press it in place. Remove the protective paper and sprinkle assorted mini beads on the exposed adhesive. Remove the excess beads. (Refer to page 24 for Bead Art.)
3. Fold small pleats in a strip of mulberry tissue and in a strip of pink fabric. Trim them to fit the bottom of the tag. (Refer to page 20 for Folding.)
4. Spray the fronts of the strips with spray adhesive and rub lightly with silver leaf paper. Tape them to the back of the tag, and add a braid and a button. (Refer to page 18 for Silver Leafing.)

Fringe Envelope

It will take only a slight breeze of nostalgia to set this showy envelope in motion.

1. Unfold a mini envelope and wrap a strip of contrasting paper around the edge of the bottom flap.
2. Cut two lengths of rayon fringe and tape them to the wrong side of the side flaps.
3. Refold the envelope and secure the ends.

Molded Ribbon

Folds of ribbon roll over this page in dramatic fashion.

1. Arrange and attach novelty papers and stickers to the page.
2. Cut a length of satin ribbon and apply a thick coat of spray adhesive to the back of the ribbon. Pinch folds in the ribbon so the coated side sticks to itself.
3. Press the flat sections of the ribbon to the paper to secure.

SIT CLOSER LOVE
for here I vow
that our 2 lives shall be as one

As long as
sea gulls love the sea

As long as
sun flowers seek the sun

MATERIALS

- 12" x 12" (30.5 x 30.5 cm) gray floral paper for the background
- solid papers: pale pink, bright pink, and teal
- print vellum
- alphabet rubber stamps
- black printing ink
- satin fabrics: blue floral and pink floral
- blue leopard faux fur
- stuffing
- satin ribbons: 1½" (3.8 cm) -wide pink stripe and 1" (2.5 cm) -wide green
- spray starch
- brads: gold and black
- black fine-point marker

HALF-MOON SETTEE

Enter this sitting room, complete with a fringed curtain and a soft settee—the perfect spot to announce an engagement.

CHOOSE PATTERNS AND TEXTURES that coordinate, but don't necessarily match. A hallmark of Victorian interiors is an eclectic mix of daring fabrics. Trim one side of the green ribbon. Cut perpendicular slits in the ribbon to make the fringe, and then hand stitch or glue the fringe to the edge of the blue floral fabric. (Refer to page 27 for Fringe.) Overlapping the edges of the background paper, arrange the blue floral fabric on the top left section of the page. Finger press folds in the satin where desired, coat the fabric with spray starch, and press. Attach the fabric to the paper with spray adhesive, and trim the edges. The templates for the settee and the heart are found on pages 180–181. Cut the heart from the pink floral satin fabric. Cut the settee from the bright pink

paper and faux fur fabric and assemble. Make the pillow by stitching together two heart shapes. Leave a small opening and turn the heart right-side-out. Stuff it lightly and stitch the opening closed. Attach it to the settee with two or three stitches and insert the gold brads along the top. Stamp the title on the print vellum and write the poem or captions on strips of pale pink paper. Cut corners from the striped satin ribbon. Noting overlaps, arrange and attach the photos, settee, paper strips, and ribbon corners to the page. Cut ¾" (1.9 cm) circles from the teal paper and secure them to the arms with black brads. Insert two more brads in the fabric folds at the top of the page.

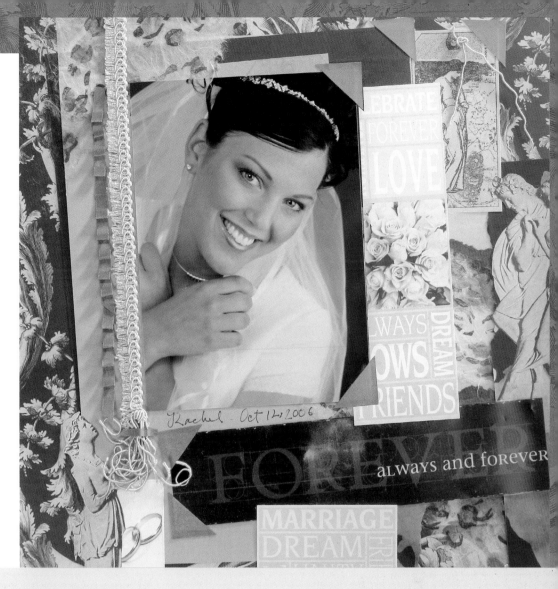

MATERIALS

- 12" x 12" (30.5 x 30.5 cm) black floral paper for the background
- solid papers: tan, black, and metallic gold
- cream mulberry tissue
- rubber eraser
- printing inks: black and tan
- novelty papers: classic figures and wedding rings
- preprinted message stickers
- preprinted title strip
- rayon braid
- rayon tassel
- black fine-point marker

ALWAYS AND FOREVER

Make a collage with many textures whose sum is greater than its parts.

PART OF THE APPEAL of this page is the monochromatic feel. The colors share the same hue and tone. Carve the eraser to make a leopard pattern and use it, along with the brown and black inks, to mark the mulberry paper. (Refer to page 23 for Leopard Print Stamps.) Let dry. Cut the tan and black solid papers into assorted rectangles and tear the print mulberry paper into sections. Trim the novelty papers and add embellishments if desired. Layer the trimmed and torn papers and the photo and attach them to the page. Trim a length of braid and attach the braid and the tassel to the page. Cut photo corners and a narrow strip from the gold metallic paper. Make folds in the strip. (Refer to page 20 for Folding.) Arrange and attach the corners, folded strip, and preprinted messages to the page. Write the caption with the marker.

COLLEGE GRADUATION, 1897

The components of this page illustrate a story of the ages—a son beginning the journey to his future.

IF YOU DON'T HAVE SILK RIBBON on hand to embellish the corner brace, use satin ribbon or paper strips. Carve the eraser to make a leopard pattern and use it, along with the brown and black inks, to mark the print paper. (Refer to page 23 for Leopard Print Stamps.) Let dry and tear the edges. The template for the decorative corner brace is found on page 182. Cut the shape from the red paper and wrap a length of silk ribbon around the long side. Tape it to the back of the corner to secure. Trim the novelty and print papers to the desired sizes. Trim the fabric and use the printer to make the title. Noting overlaps, arrange and attach the papers, fabric, decorative corner, and photos to the page. Attach a selected photo with foam adhesive spacers to add dimension. Also attach the title, die cut, and brads to the page.

MATERIALS

- 12" x 12" (30.5 x 30.5 cm) red floral paper for the background
- solid papers: red and cream
- green print paper
- rubber eraser
- printing inks: black and tan
- novelty papers: script and typed copy
- floral die cut
- silk ribbon
- leopard print fabric
- dragonfly brads
- foam adhesive spacers
- computer printer

MATERIALS

- 12" x 12" (30.5 x 30.5 cm) chocolate paper for background
- blue brushed paper
- cherub print vellum
- antique paper frames
- peacock feathers
- library envelopes
- dye: green and magenta
- ribbon: brown satin and cream rayon
- paper tag
- red rayon thread
- lavender mulberry tissue
- jewel brads
- preprinted caption strips
- assorted paper scraps of coordinating colors
- white colored pencil

PEACOCK FEATHERS

Show off your favorite faces and ephemera. Then top it off with resplendent feathers and crimped fringe.

CHOOSE WHICH ONE of the many eye-catching details on this page is your favorite. Tear the edge of the blue brushed paper and cut the faces from the cherub vellum. Noting overlaps, arrange and attach the papers, photo, frames, and feathers to the page. Trim any overlapping edges. Cut a length of ribbon and pull the horizontal thread from one cut end to unravel. Since the weave is directional, one cut end will unravel more easily than the other. Attach the ribbon to the page. Cut 3" (7.6 cm) circles from the mulberry tissue. Referring to the Yo-Yo Flowers on page 30, stitch and trim the circles to make flowers. Cut a short length of ribbon and unravel one cut end, leaving ½" (1.3 cm) of ribbon intact. Cut a small slit in the remaining ribbon and in the center of one flower. Layer the flower on the ribbon end and secure to the page with a brad. Repeat with the remaining ribbon and flower. Mix the dyes to the desired strengths and dip the envelopes in the dyes. (Refer to page 144 for Dip-Dyed Paper.) Let dry and insert the caption strips and paper scraps in the envelopes. Wrap one with the cream ribbon and attach the paper tag. Trim the paper scraps and wrap one scrap strip with the rayon thread. Arrange and attach the paper scraps and envelopes to the page. Use the pencil to write the title.

MATERIALS

- 12" x 12" (30.5 x 30.5 cm) green print paper for the background
- paper frame
- pressed flowers (Refer to page 22 for Pressed Flowers)
- alphabet stickers
- antique postcard and stamp

WE WERE FRAMED

Balance bold stickers with bold, look-you-straight-in-the-eye photos.

PRESSED FLOWERS ARE FRAGILE and sometimes they will lose petals, so be sure to handle them delicately. As you would with confetti, sprinkle loose petals on the corners or edges of the page. Also, keep scale and balance in mind when mixing and matching eclectic alphabet letters. Noting overlaps, arrange and attach the photos, frame, postcard, and stamp to the page. Press the stickers in place. Arrange and attach the dried flowers and leaves to the page. This composition proves that sometimes the best-looking pages are the easiest to make.

MATERIALS

- 12" x 12" (30.5 x 30.5 cm) papers: pale pink and pink print vellum for the background
- solid papers: pink and lavender
- lavender tissue
- cream mulberry tissue
- adhesive-back craft foam
- flower border
- green eyelets
- assorted brads
- alphabet stickers
- alphabet rub-ons
- preprinted message strips

SURPRISE PACKAGE

A hopscotch page of words and images proves that presentation is everything.

AN OVERLAY OF VELLUM makes these carved designs bubble up through the surface of the page. The template for the carved flower is found on page 182. Cut the shapes from the craft foam and press them in place on the pink background paper. (Refer to page 21 for Carved Details.) Tear strips from the mulberry tissue and use them to cover the foam flowers. Cut shaped windows in the vellum paper and attach it to the pink paper. The concave edges of the windows will require extra adhesive. Attach the lavender tissue of the flower centers to the page with small brads. Attach the floral border to the page and add eyelet details. Cut a large rectangle from the lavender paper for the name box and small strips from the lavender and pink papers to place behind the messages. Arrange and attach them to the page. Press the stickers in place and apply the rub-on letters. Secure the clear message strips over the paper strips with the remaining brads.

Tag Anthology

How do I love tags? Let me count the ways...

THE COMPLETED PAGE is a collection of individually decorated tags. Make tags similar to those on the photo model, or design your own. Cover several tags with appliqués and mini beads. (Refer to page 24 for Bead Art.) Wrap two tags with rayon ribbon. Wrap a tag with tulle and wind floss through the netting. Decorate the remaining tags with novelty papers, cloth, paper stickers, and charms. Cut a triangle from the fabric. Arrange and attach the fabric, tags, and photo to the page. Write captions on strips of notebook paper and attach them to the page with brads.

Materials

- 12" x 12" (30.5 x 30.5 cm) rust print paper for the background
- paper tags
- tag embellishments: mini beads, rayon ribbon, velvet ribbon, embroidered appliqués, eyelets, tulle, fabric alphabet stickers, and novelty papers
- leopard print fabric
- notebook paper
- fine-point black marker
- brads
- charms
- floss

MATERIALS

- 12" x 12" (30.5 x 30.5 cm) pink paper for the background

- solid papers: white, pale pink, and melon

- embossed paper

- spatter paper

- pink quilling strips

- landscape rubber stamps

- black printing ink

- paper flowers

- eyelets: silver and lavender

- fine-gauge silver wire

- decorator chalk

- white rayon ribbon

- mini pearl strands

- acrylic paint: gray, white, and pink

- computer printer

A special day for Catherine and for the bride and groom - Lindsay and Hugh

FLOWER GIRL AND FRETWORK

Settle in beneath the unbeatable architecture of coils and pearls.

MIXING MANY MEDIA and techniques keeps the eye moving smoothly around the page. The templates for the corner brackets are found on page 183. For the large bracket, cut the background from the melon paper and the detail from the white paper. Use the acrylic paints to marbleize the detail section. (Refer to page 16 for Marbling.) Let dry. Insert the eyelets in the bracket and the paper flowers. Cut the small bracket from the pale pink paper. Make coils of assorted sizes from the quilling strips. (Refer to page 25 for Quilled Paper.) Glue the coils to the small bracket. Let dry. Tear irregular shapes from the embossed paper and shade them with the decorator chalk. Print the landscape designs on the white paper and let dry. Cut two lengths of ribbon and spray the backs with spray adhesive. Arrange them with folds and twists if desired and press them in place on the page. Cut a small irregular shape from the spatter paper. Noting overlaps, arrange and attach the white paper, photo, embossed paper, print papers, spatter paper, and brackets on the page. Thread lengths of wire through the paper flowers and loop the opposite ends through the bracket eyelets. Twist together the wire ends to secure them. Outline sections of the large bracket with pearl strands. Print the title and attach it to the page.

MATERIALS

- 12" x 12" (30.5 x 30.5 cm) red poinsettia paper for the background
- print papers: green striped, green spatter, and green heart print
- quilt novelty paper
- large snowflake die cuts
- stickers: small snowflakes and birds
- antique postcards
- preprinted title strip
- bugle beads
- fine-gauge wire
- double-sided adhesive strips
- black fine-point marker

THE BEST GIFT

Echo the sparkle in these eyes with rows of shiny bugle beads.

THE BEADS ON THE PHOTO MODEL are arranged in a chevron design. You can also make stripes or squares with the ordered strands. Trim the quilt and spatter papers to the desired sizes. Noting overlaps, arrange and attach the quilt and spatter papers, postcards, photo, and die-cut snowflakes to the page. Cut the striped paper into vertical strips. Layer them and, leaving the bottom edges free, attach them to the page. Slightly curl up the bottom edges. Press the stickers in place. Cut a length of wire and, leaving 2" (5.1 cm) at each end, thread the desired number of beads on the wire. (Refer to page 24 for Bead Art.) Repeat to make a total of seven strands. Cover one side of the adhesive strips with the green heart print paper. Place the strands side by side on the page and press a strip of covered adhesive on each set of ends to secure. Trim the wire ends and/or wrap them to the back of the page. Attach the preprinted title and write the caption with the marker.

MATERIALS

- 12" x 12" (30.5 x 30.5 cm) papers: purple, purple print, and purple scroll paper for the background
- solid papers: pink and white
- brushed silver paper
- print papers: large floral, lavender crackle, purple scroll, and purple crackle
- lavender tissue
- vine rubber stamp
- blue stamping ink
- fine-gauge wire: silver and magenta
- micro beads: yellow, pink, magenta, and blue
- pink rayon tassel
- computer printer

Behind the Scenes at Shawn's Wedding

Avery, Scott, and T.J.

BUTTERFLY WISHES

Wishes for a happy future take flight in the form of fluttering butterflies and corkscrew wire.

MICRO BEADS ARE AVAILABLE in a wide variety of colors and finishes. Combine glass and metal beads to create an interesting grain on a paper fan. Tear the top corner from the purple scroll paper and attach it the purple paper. Tear sections from the tissue and stamp vines on the sections. Let dry. Cut arcs of various lengths from the lavender and purple crackle papers. Noting overlaps, arrange and attach the tissue, photos, and arcs to the page. Cut lengths of silver and magenta wire and shape them into loops and coils. Attach the wires to the page with ½" (1.3 cm) lengths of tape. The template for the butterfly is found on page 184. Cut six butterflies from the silver paper and attach them to the page covering the tape. The template for the fan is found on page 184. From the floral paper, cut a fan and mark and crease the folds. Cut and attach sections from the double-sided adhesive sheet that match the colored sections on the fan. (Refer to page 24 for Bead Art.) Remove the protective paper from one area and sprinkle beads on the exposed adhesive. Repeat the process for the remaining colors. Place narrow strips of double-sided adhesive to the straight sides of the fan. Attach the fan to the page with the folds intact and the top edge of the fan covering the wire ends. Cut the fan base (template is found on page 184) from the pink paper and fold the sides. Slip the end of the pink rayon tassel under the base and attach it to the page with double-sided adhesive. Print the title on the white paper. Trim, and attach it to the page.

Sasha suffering from a serious case of Flower Girl anxiety

MATERIALS
- 12" x 12" (30.5 x 30.5 cm) papers: pink print and rust print for the background
- solid papers: chocolate, copper, and white
- vellum: white and white-on-white print
- print papers: green marble and purple scroll
- print paper mat
- flower photos (clipped from magazines or catalogs)
- gold velvet rayon
- printed title box
- butterfly stamps
- computer printer
- organza ribbon

UNTIE THE RIBBON

Unravel the edges of a rayon patch to make an accent with a fluid, organic feel.

To make the unraveling process easier, try tossing the cut fabric swatches in the washing machine. Trim ½" (1.3 cm) from the left edge of the rust print paper and attach it to the pink paper. Cut a rectangle from the fabric that is 2" (5.1 cm) larger on all sides than the paper mat. Carefully pull the threads from the edges of the rectangle and trim the frayed edges to create an uneven border. (Refer to page 27 for Fringe.) Make a layered mat with the purple scroll paper, fabric, and marble paper. Cut strips from the solid papers and vellum, and cut a rectangle from the copper paper. Noting overlaps, arrange and attach the trimmed papers, title box, mat, photo, and flower photos to the page. Press the stamps in place. Print the caption on the white paper, trim, and attach it to the page. Cover the caption with the organza ribbon.

MATERIALS

- 12" x 12" (30.5 x 30.5 cm) pale pink paper for the background
- solid papers: light blue, light pink, and medium pink
- pink herringbone paper
- vellum: white, vine print, and floral print
- novelty papers: green disks and flowers
- quilling strips: pink and blue
- white tissue paper
- wedding announcement
- white tulle
- fine-gauge wire: silver and green
- rubber stamps: script, flower, and alphabet
- stamping inks: blue and green
- silver ricrac
- jewel brads
- silver leaf paper
- colored pencils

UPSTAIRS/DOWNSTAIRS

Represent two floors and two moods on one page.

A WHIMSICAL STAIRCASE is the backdrop for a bride's stunning entrance. Stamp the script on the background paper; let dry. The templates for the handrails are on page 185. Cut handrails from the blue paper and rectangles for the stairs from the pink and herringbone papers. Arrange and attach cut shapes to page. Stamp flowers on white vellum, let dry, then color with pencils. Cut corners from the vine vellum and cut flowers from the floral vellum. Stamp captions on the tissue and trim. Attach vellum sections, photos, announcement, stamped flowers, and novelty flower paper to the page. Attach captions and short lengths of ricrac to the page. Cut 2" (5.1 cm) -wide strips from the tulle and fold the long sides in to the centers. Pierce the paper on both sides of the handrail

with a needle and secure the tulle over the handrail by threading the green wire through the holes. Use the pencils to draw the title on the white vellum. Cut a flower from double-sided adhesive that matches the stamp and use it to secure title to the page. Remove protective paper and rub silver leaf paper on the exposed adhesive. Brush away excess silver leaf with a cotton swab or soft brush. (Refer to page 18 for Silver Leafing.) Cut quilling strips into 4" (10.2 cm) lengths, make coils, and glue to the page. (Refer to page 25 for Quilled Paper.) Make wire coils and attach with narrow strips of double-sided adhesive. Cover exposed adhesive with bits of tissue paper. Insert brads in the paper disks and attach them to the page.

MATERIALS

- 12" x 12" (30.5 x 30.5 cm) purple paper for the background
- vellum: script and floral
- tissue paper: silver and lavender
- silver metallic paper
- print Mylar border
- small shaped mat
- small print mat
- frames: two white embossed and one silver
- small items for inside the frames: print flower, stitched mirror, wire monogram, and charm
- two lengths of pink metal chain with fasteners

ROOM WITH A VIEW

Complete with pleated curtains, a dreamy setting creeps in on little cat feet.

REPLACE THE MYLAR BORDER with a title or a caption if you desire. To make the page, tear a large rectangle from the script vellum and tear small scraps from the floral vellum and lavender tissue. Arrange and attach the rectangles, border, and photo to the page. Tear a small rectangle from the silver paper. Place the shaped mat on the page. Coat the back of the silver paper with spray adhesive and press it in place over the mat. Layer and attach the small print mat, the frames, and assorted small items to the page. Make the strips used on the corners by covering double-sided adhesive with colored paper.

Cut two rectangles from the silver tissue for the curtains. Cut them to the desired length and twice the desired width. Pinch small folds at the top edges for pleats. Place strips of double-sided adhesive at the top corners of the photo and small squares of adhesive at the bottom edges of the curtains. Press the pleats over the adhesive at the tops of the curtains. Make loose folds at the bottom edges and press in place on the squares. Pierce small holes in the paper and attach the chains to the page as tiebacks.

MATERIALS

- 12" x 12" (30.5 x 30.5 cm) lavender print paper for the background
- black paper
- assorted paper scraps of coordinating prints and colors
- die-cut bows: black and white
- two garters
- two paper tags
- small items to embellish the tags: postcards, paper scraps, stamps, stickers, mini envelopes, embroidered appliqués, and charms
- scraps of assorted blue print cotton fabrics
- stitched trim with adhesive back
- preprinted title boxes
- alphabet stickers
- caption strip
- white colored pencil

SISTER ACT

What remains when the day is done are bits and pieces of shared memories.

THE CRAZY-QUILT BACKGROUND of the photo model is made with only fabric. Feel free to mix in paper patches with the fabric ones. Trim the print papers to the desired shapes. Noting overlaps, arrange and attach them to the page. Trim the fabric scraps into small shapes that measure between 1" (2.5 cm) and 2½" (6.4 cm). (Refer to page 19 for Crazy Quilt Piecing.) Coat the backs of the scraps with spray adhesive and, overlapping the edges, attach them to the page. Trim the fabric scraps flush with the page edges. Cut narrow strips

from the desired fabric and, forming a jagged line, attach them along the edge of the quilt design. Attach the photo to the page. Create coils and loops with the stitched trim and press it in place on the page. Trim the ends. Decorate the tags and attach them to the garters. Cut a curved strip from the black paper for the caption. Noting overlaps, arrange and attach the die-cut bows, tags, title box, stickers, and caption strip to the page. Use the white pencil to write the caption.

- 12" x 12" (30.5 x 30.5 cm) papers: green, white, and green print for the background
- white paper
- white vellum
- quilling strips: pink and yellow
- folded paper fans
- Victorian decoupage papers
- print feathers
- acrylic paint
- computer printer

FLIGHTS OF FANCY

Feathers and fans show off this child in grand style.

MAKE YOUR OWN FOLDED FANS if you can't find the size and style that coordinate with your embellishments. The template for the cut edge is found on page 186. Cut the edges in the white and the green print papers. Layer and attach the trimmed paper and photo to the page. Spray the backs of the feathers with the spray adhesive and attach them to the page. Cut 4" (10.2 cm) lengths from the pink quilling paper. (Refer to page 25 for Quilled Paper.) Coil and pinch the strips to make flower petals. Cut the yellow quilling paper to various lengths and fold the lengths to make flower centers, leaves, and stems. Using small dots of white craft glue, attach the flowers, stems, and leaves to the page. Cut the letters for the title from the white paper and paint them. Let dry. Print the remaining part of the title and attach both sections to the page. Tape a strip of vellum over the selected part of the title. Attach the decoupage papers and the fans to the page.

MATERIALS

- 12" x 12" (30.5 x 30.5 cm) black print paper for the background
- print papers: black umbrella print and gray crackle
- brown paper strips
- gray vellum strips
- die-cut vase with flowers
- flower novelty paper
- alphabet rubber stamps
- black printing ink
- fibers for fringe: olive and light green embroidery floss, rust rayon ribbon, and green fuzzy yarn
- black sequins

MOTHER AND SON

Lose the bulk of fringed cord but keep the swing with fringed paper strips.

EXPERIMENT WITH ADDITIONAL FRINGE materials such as rayon thread or knitting yarn. Cut a wide strip from the umbrella paper and a rectangle from the crackle paper. Cut a small square from the novelty paper. Cut short lengths of yarn and tape the ends to the back of the vase. Noting overlaps, arrange and attach the trimmed papers, photo, and vase with flowers. Stamp the title on the vellum strips. Let dry. Punch holes along the edges of the brown paper strips. Cut short lengths of the assorted fibers and loop them through the holes to make fringe. (Refer to page 27 for Fringe.) Arrange and attach the fringe strips, title strips, and sequins to the page.

Grandpa Jake was born on the ship that brought his family to America.

His older sisters made lace at a large warehouse in New York City. They each brought him a piece of candy when they got home from work.

MATERIALS

- 12" x 12" (30.5 x 30.5 cm) papers: tan print and white for the background
- print papers: green stripes and flowers
- solid papers: gold and white
- tea
- pink vellum
- paper corners
- flower die cut
- cream mulberry tissue
- adhesive-back craft foam
- glass beads: gold and lavender
- decorative corners
- script Mylar box
- computer printer

THE IMMIGRANT SONG

Cast a long shadow with old photos and high impact carving.

PLACE A LARGE DESIGN ELEMENT off center on your page and weight the opposite side with photos and small accents. Trim 1½" (3.8 cm) from the top of the white paper and attach it to the tan print paper. The template for the scroll pattern is found on page 187. Cut the shapes from the craft foam and press them in place on the page. (Refer to page 21 for Carved Details.) Cover the shapes with the mulberry tissue. Cut a curved strip from the tissue and hand stitch the beads in a random pattern to secure. (Refer to page 24 for

Bead Art.) Cut small strips of the striped paper, gold paper, and flower paper. Cut or tear small shapes from the vellum. Noting overlaps, arrange and attach the scraps, strips, photos, corners, and die cut to the page. Also attach the beaded strip and the script Mylar box to the page. Print the title and the caption on the white paper. Dip them in tea to age them. (Refer to page 26 for Tea-Dyed Paper.) Let dry, press, and trim. Attach the title and the caption to the page.

MATERIALS

- 12" x 12" (30.5 x 30.5 cm) light pink paper for the background
- solid papers: white and brown
- novelty papers: tile and text
- old book
- bookmark
- ribbon: wide blue satin, brown print grosgrain, and pink silk
- cherry rubber stamp
- brown printing ink
- embroidery floss: pink, green, and rust
- paper tag
- paper roses
- acrylic paint: pink, blue, brown, and gray
- black colored pencil

BIOGRAPHY

This new release is sure to make the best-seller list.

FRAME THE PRINCESS in this fairy tale with an altered art book cover. Use the acrylic paints to marbleize the white paper. (Refer to page 16 for Marbling.) Let dry. Cut the paper into sections and attach them to the page. Cut individual tiles from the tile paper and sections from the text paper. Noting overlaps, arrange and attach the paper tiles, text, and photo to the page. Using a craft knife, carefully cut the cover from the book along the binding edge. Cut a window in the cover. It will take several passes with the craft knife to cut through the cover. Decorate the cover by taping the roses to the inside of the window and a strip of the bookmark along the side. Tie a length of pink ribbon around the bottom. Cut the brown ribbon into small squares and attach them to the corners of the tiles. Stamp the cherries on several lengths of the blue ribbon and let dry. Embroider selected cherries. (Refer to page 95 for Embroidery.) Place the cover and stamped ribbon lengths on the page and piece the ribbon together to fit around the marbled paper, paper tiles, and cover. Attach the ribbon lengths and cover to the page. Thread assorted floss colors through the paper tag and secure the tag to the page with paper-covered strips of double-sided adhesive. Cut the tile from the brown paper and attach it to the page. Use the colored pencil to write a message.

MATERIALS

- 12" x 12" (30.5 x 30.5 cm) navy paper for the background
- silver brushed paper
- mauve mottle paper
- novelty quilt paper
- antique postcard
- stickers: cloud, stamp, and alphabet
- stamp stickers
- paper tag
- pink tulle
- silver keys
- heart-shaped brads

A GENTLE AGE

Piece together a patchwork of exotic stamps, burnished charms, and family photos.

IF YOUR ANTIQUE PHOTOS are dissimilar sizes, resize them with a commercial scanning and printing machine found at a photo store or a copy center. The template for the frame sections is found on page 187. Note that the template will make a frame with a 2¾" (7 cm) window. Adjust the length of the template to fit your photo(s). From the silver paper, cut four sections for each frame, and mark and crease the folds. (Refer to page 20 for Folding.) Cut mauve squares that are larger than the folded frames. Center the photo(s) on the squares and attach the frame sections with strips of double-sided adhesive. Cut strips from the quilt paper and attach them to the page. Press the cloud and stamp stickers in place. Trim the postcard and attach the postcard and photos to the page. Cut a strip of tulle and thread the ends through the paper tag. Attach the tulle ends and the keys to the page. Press the alphabet stickers in place for the title and caption. Insert the brads in the frames.

MATERIALS

- 12" x 12" (30.5 x 30.5 cm) papers: black and lavender flocked for the background
- white paper
- taupe mottle paper
- silver tissue paper
- preprinted title box
- silver eyelets
- white organza ribbon
- computer printer

A ROUND OF APPLAUSE, PLEASE

Encircled with love and ruffles, this lucky couple begins a life together.

USE MATCHING OR CONTRASTING THREAD to stitch the gathering seam, and pull the bottom thread because it is looser and easier to gather. Tear opposite corners from the flocked paper and attach the flocked paper to the black paper. Trim the taupe paper. Insert eyelets in three of the corners of the photo, then cut short lengths of ribbon and loop them through the eyelets. Cut ¾" (1.9 cm) -wide lengths of tissue paper. With the sewing machine, run a gathering stitch down the centers and gather them to the desired length and fullness. (Refer to page 17 for Ruching.) Place the taupe paper, photo, and title box on the page and arrange the gathered strips over and under the edges. Attach them to the page. Print the caption on the white paper and trim and attach the title and caption to the page.

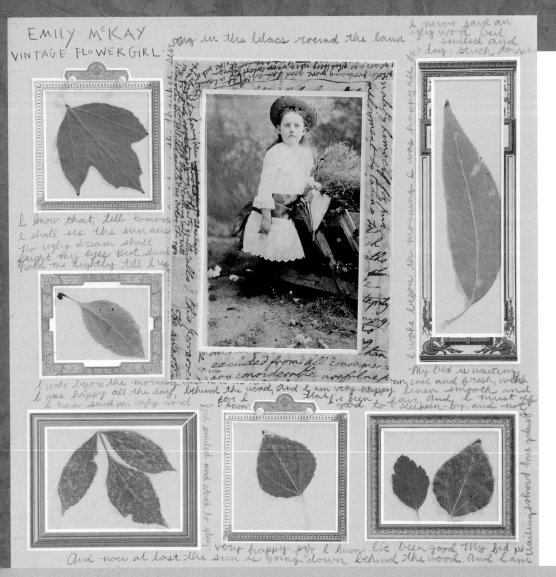

GALLERY GARDEN

Bring out the artist in you and display your leaf collection in gallery frames.

MATERIALS

- 12" x 12" (30.5 x 30.5 cm) pink paper for the background
- assorted paper mats
- dried leaves (Refer to page 22 for Pressed Flowers)
- small brads
- colored pencils: navy and brown

TRY PLACING BEHIND THE MATS other small objects such as bits of ribbon, lace, or small paper ephemera. Place the small mats on the page and center the leaves behind them. Lightly mark the page for leaf placement. Coat the backs of the leaves with spray adhesive and gently press them in place. Remove any pencil marks. Attach the photo and mats to the page. Insert the brads in the selected mats. Write the title and text with the colored pencils.

MATERIALS

- 12" x 12" (30.5 x 30.5 cm) khaki print paper for the background
- taupe paper
- print stitched paper
- assorted paper scraps of coordinating prints and colors
- flower novelty paper
- antique birthday card
- brass paper clip
- brass coins
- scraps of assorted exotic fabrics
- alphabet stickers
- preprinted title box and caption strip
- copper leaf paper

COPPER QUILT BIRTHDAY

The hallmark of graceful aging is an attractive patina.

FORGET THE CAKE AND CANDLES—mark the passing of another year with an artful quilt border. Trim the photo where desired and trim the taupe paper to create a shadow. Piece together paper scraps and attach the trimmed paper and photo to the papers. Cut a strip from the stitched paper and cut rectangles from the scrap papers. Noting overlaps, arrange and attach the strip, rectangles, and layered photo to the page. Trim the fabric scraps into small shapes that measure between 1" (2.5 cm) and 2½" (6.4 cm). (Refer to page 19 for Crazy Quilt Piecing.) Coat the backs of the scraps with spray adhesive and, overlapping the edges, attach them to the page. Trim any overlapping edges. Make adhesive-backed paper strips and use them to cover selected seams. Thread paper strips through the paper clip and coins and attach them to the page. Mask the flower paper, birthday card, and title box. Coat only the corners with spray adhesive. (Refer to page 18 for Silver Leafing.) Place the copper leaf paper over the adhesive and rub. Peel the leaf paper from the corners. Press the stickers in place and attach the flower paper, card, title box, and caption strip to the page.

Looking forward to a lifetime of toast and hot chocolate together

MATERIALS

- 12" x 12" (30.5 x 30.5 cm) cream print paper for the background
- white paper
- assorted paper scraps of coordinating prints and colors
- fine-gauge gold wire
- assorted mini beads
- white organza ribbon
- black eyelets
- assorted brads
- die cuts: flowers, windows, and butterfly
- satin gloves
- computer printer
- black fine-point marker

LOOKING FORWARD TOGETHER

No ordinary edge, this border is made of organza layers, beads, and mini wedding relics.

TWO OF THE THREE BEAD STRANDS are made with loops that resemble small flowers. To form a loop, thread several beads on the wire and then loop the end back through them. Continue beading as desired. Trim the scrap papers to the desired sizes. Noting overlaps, arrange and attach the papers, photos, and flower die cuts to the page. Cut or tear small sections from the remaining papers and attach them, along with the window and butterfly die cuts, to the page. Cut a length of ribbon and, creating small folds under each eyelet, secure it to the page. Cut three lengths of wire and, leaving 3" (7.6 cm) at each end, thread the selected beads on the wires. (Refer to page 24 for Bead Art.) Note that two lengths are threaded with small loops. Shape the beaded wires and secure the ends to the page with small brads. Trim the wire ends. Print the title insert on the white paper. Trim around the words and attach the insert and gloves to the page. Use the marker to finish writing the title.

MATERIALS

- 12" x 12" (30.5 x 30.5 cm) rust print paper for the background
- assorted paper scraps of coordinating prints and colors
- solid papers: purple, bronze, and tan
- novelty papers: horse, assorted script, tiles, medallions, and buttons
- print papers: blue and purple
- antique postcard
- rust embroidery floss
- preprinted caption strip
- coins
- stitched trim with adhesive back
- green rayon cord
- brown marker

ONE-ROOM SCHOOLHOUSE

Take a peek at an amber and aged day-in-the-life-of page.

PLACING AN ENGAGING PHOTO under draping curves creates a keyhole effect that invites you to take a closer look. Make the second look more meaningful by adding life snippets of parents, pets, and collections. Trim selected scrap papers, script, and horse papers to the desired sizes. Trim the postcard. Noting overlaps, arrange and attach the caption strip, trimmed papers, postcard, and photos to the page. Cut a corner shape from the bronze paper. Cut small strips and squares from the tile paper, and use the floss to hand stitch them to the border. (Refer to page 147 for Stitched Paper.) Cut the medallion paper into squares. Attach the medallions, stitched border, and coins to the page. Lightly mark the curves for the trim on the page. Cut the stitched trim to desired lengths and press it in place on the marked lines. Cut a length of cord. Slightly untwist the ends and stitch the ends of the strands to the page to secure. Cut strips with irregular borders from the blue print paper. (Refer to page 20 for Folding.) Fold the strips. Cut narrow strips from the purple print paper and back them with double-sided adhesive. Press the narrow strips over the folded strips to hold the folds in place. Attach the folded strips and a torn corner of tan paper to the page. Use the marker to write the title.

MATERIALS

- 12" x 12" (30.5 x 30.5 cm) tan print paper for the background
- solid papers: black, white, copper, bronze, gray, and green
- light green crackle paper
- bronze tissue
- green vellum
- novelty papers: copy, script, cherub, and engraved
- assorted print mats
- stamps
- metal label holder
- small brads
- rub-on caption
- cream mulberry tissue
- adhesive-back craft foam
- copper leaf paper
- alphabet rubber stamps
- black printing ink
- computer printer
- tea

BABY'S DAY OUT

Commemorate a toddler's day of big-city discovery with a mixed bag of textures and finishes.

THE PERFECT VICTORIAN COMPOSITION appears to be halfway between order and disarray. Arrange and then rearrange your component parts to achieve this effect. Cut strips from the copper paper, bronze tissue, and green crackle paper. Arrange and attach the trimmed papers on the page. The template for the tree is found on page 188. Cut the trunk from the copper and the bronze papers, the tree top from the green vellum, and the individual leaves from the gray and green papers. Mount selected photos on black paper and trim. Cut small sections from the novelty papers. Noting overlaps, arrange and attach the paper mats, tree, photos, and novelty papers. Attach the label holder with the brads. Cut 1¼" x ⅝" (3.1 x 1.6 cm) bricks from the craft foam. Press them in place on the page. (Refer to page 21 for Carved Details.) Cover the shapes with the mulberry tissue. Cover selected bricks with rubber cement and let dry. (Refer to page 18 for Silver Leafing.) Cover the bricks with the copper leaf paper and rub. Carefully remove the copper leaf paper. Attach the stamps to the page and rub on the caption. Stamp the first word of the title. Print the remaining words for the title on the white paper. Dip them in tea to age them. (Refer to page 26 for Tea-Dyed Paper.) Let dry, press, trim, and attach them to the page.

MATERIALS

- 12" x 12" (30.5 x 30.5 cm) pink print paper for the background
- solid papers: white, pink, and black
- bronze paper
- floral print papers
- medallion die cut
- aged book pages
- landscape rubber stamps
- brown printing ink
- colored pencils
- gold satin ribbon with wire edges
- brown print grosgrain ribbon
- gold wire
- garland embellishments: gray ribbon, stickers, a gem, a sequin, and assorted charms
- embroidery floss: green and gold
- preprinted captions
- computer printer

LONG AGO AND NOT SO FAR AWAY

String together a variety of lighthearted garlands.

THE STERN EXPRESSIONS of long-ago faces often belie the real romance of their lives. Soften the mood with garlands of fringe and jewels. Stamp the landscapes on the white paper. Let dry. Color them with the colored pencils and trim or tear around the images. Cut photo corners from the floral and bronze papers. Cut a small rectangle from the floral paper and strips from the book pages. Noting overlaps, arrange and attach the stamped images, rectangle and strips, photos, photo corners, and medallion to the page. Cut various lengths from the gold and brown ribbons. Make fringe from each by unraveling the cut edge or by tying short strips of gray ribbon around them. (Refer to page 27 for Fringe.) Another technique consists of cutting short perpendicular strips in the ribbon and pulling away the cut fibers. Cut two lengths of gold wire. Hang the stickers, gem, sequin, and charms from the wire with loops of embroidery floss. The template for the scallop is found on page 188. Cut one scallop from the bronze paper. Shape and twist the ribbons and wire and attach them to the page with the narrow strips of double-sided adhesive. Print the titles on the pink paper. Tape them to torn strips of the book pages and trim. Attach them to the page with short strips of black paper. Attach the captions to the page.

RETRO STYLE: THE '50S

WITH WORLD WAR II OVER, and the world shifting and settling, soldiers became construction workers and businessmen. They found brides, moved to the suburbs for lives of domestic bliss, and shared a common goal of returning the world to a place that was nurturing and safe. On a national scale, there was an explosion of babies being born and mothers needed something to do while the babies napped and the kids were at school. Amusing themselves by learning skills, such as needlework and decorative painting, they made things to decorate their homes and took pride in their handiwork.

In order to drive back and forth from the suburbs, you had to have a car. Travel became an obsession, and as a result, diners and amusement parks popped up like mushrooms along the roadsides.

The styles of the day had an unmistakable innocence to them. Illustrations in picture books had soft edges and accompanied stories of lost puppies and marching ducks. Because of this tender attitude, many of the projects in this chapter include visual references to toys and play.

When scrapping in this style, use friendly patterns and color combinations. Anything pink will work. And be sure to add travel-related backgrounds and novelty papers when appropriate. Look for papers that picture exotic or quirky landmarks. I am looking for a patch or border touting the "world's biggest ball of string" for my next '50s composition.

For 1950s style, think poodle haircuts, poodle skirts, and anything French (including the Eiffel Tower and, yes, poodles). Flowers are the pattern of choice, followed by the buttoned-down polka dot. Go soft and subtle—with a nod to conformity—by choosing neutral colors with a splash of pink. The decade of interstate highways and television opened up the world, so celebrate by noting famous tourist attractions and regional landmarks.

technique:
STENCILING

Stenciling is an art form that is centuries old, but it enjoyed special popularity during the '50s. A versatile form of surface decoration, stenciled designs are broken up into flat areas of color. Then a stencil is cut for each color and paint is applied in the negative spaces of each. It requires no special skill and can be used to make multiple images. Used most often to decorate linens, trendy '50s motifs included chickens and baked goods for the kitchen and exotic birds and animals for the dining room.

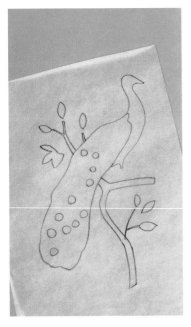

STEP 1

Draw the design on tracing paper.

STEP 2

Cut one stencil for each color. Use heavy paper, stencil plastic, or Mylar for the stencils and clean them after each use.

STEP 3

Place the stencil on the page and hold it securely with one hand. Dip the end of the stenciling brush in the paint and blot it on a paper towel. Apply the paint in the exposed area with short up and down pouncing strokes. Remove the stencil and let dry.

STEP 4

Repeat Step 3 for the remaining colors and add details with a pencil or a marker.

See the projects on pages 75, 76, 84, 86, 101, 109, and 111 that feature Stenciling.

technique:
MACARONI ART

Macaroni art—an oxymoron? Maybe, but if you are familiar with these spirited kitchen mosaics made from colored macaroni, you will agree it was the quirkiest trend of the decade. Framed compositions of pasta and glue most definitely put the kitsch in kitchen. Use small shapes such as ancini di pepe, mini bow ties, or mini flowers, or pasta with a low profile such as spaghetti. Use fabric dye, food coloring, or watercolor paint for dye and white craft glue to cement the pieces to the page.

STEP 1

Dilute the food coloring and immerse the pasta in the dye. Allow the pasta to soak for only thirty seconds to a minute so it doesn't soften or break down.

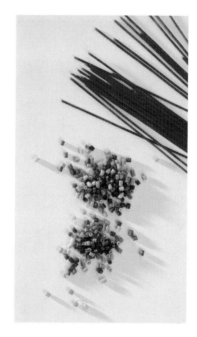

STEP 2

Remove the pasta from the dye and allow it to dry.

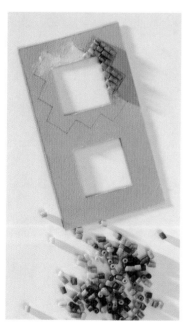

STEP 3

Draw the design on the page with a pencil. Working in small areas, cover the paper with white craft glue and place the pasta within the designated area. Let dry.

STEP 4

Trim or tear around the design edge or leave a paper border around the edge of the pasta.

See the projects on pages 76, 81, and 85 that feature Macaroni Art.

technique:
FINGER PAINT

The most primitive way to manipulate paint is with your fingers, and smooth finger paint is what many of us used to make our first masterpieces. Since genuine finger paint is too thick for scrapbook applications, use this recipe adapted for flat pages. It provides the same even color but has enough translucence and body to retain finger strokes. For best results, apply light paint to dark paper and dark paint to light paper.

STEP 1

Mix one part liquid poster paint with one part liquid starch.

STEP 2

Drip the paint on the page.

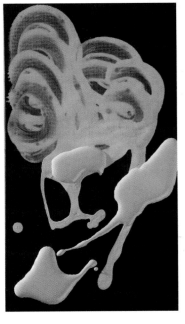

STEP 3

Use your fingertips to make swirls or waves in the paint. Let dry.

STEP 4

After the paint has dried it may be necessary to press the paper to flatten it. If so, place the paper right side down on the work surface and cover it with a sheet of typing paper before pressing.

See the projects on pages 80 and 85 that feature Finger Paint.

technique:
BRAIDING

Children in the '50s spent their afternoons lying on braided rugs and watching Roy Rogers ride off into a glorious sunset of black and white. Use the same braided strands that made up the rugs to dress up your pages. The braiding technique is the same, but two different materials can be used, with distinctly different results. Paper braids are flat and stiff, and can be creased or folded. Fabric braids have a soft, fluid look and can be coiled like a rug. They also can be embellished by stitching buttons or beads onto the braided strands.

STEP 1 FOR PAPER

Tape together the ends of paper strips and secure the taped end to the edge of a table or countertop. As you braid, fold the edges of the strips at an angle to create an even edge.

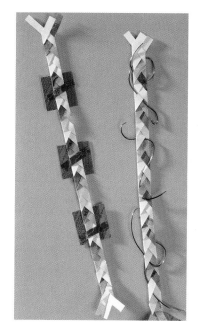

STEP 2 FOR PAPER

After braiding, tape the loose ends together. Decorate the braided strands with paper accents or wire.

STEP 1 FOR FABRIC

Stitch together the ends of the fabric strips and secure the stitched end to the edge of a table or countertop.

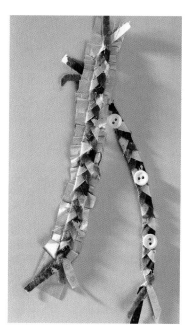

STEP 2 FOR FABRIC

After braiding, stitch the loose ends together. Decorate the braided strands with gathered tissue paper or buttons.

See the projects on pages 75, 83, and 87 that feature Braiding.

technique:
CHENILLE

Why have '50s bathrobes become collector's items? Because they are covered with lush chenille and graphic motifs. The chenille of vintage bathrobes was made by stitching loops of cotton floss through a cotton backing. The loops were clipped and the fabric was washed in hot water to shrink the threads around the stitches. Imitate the unique texture of chenille with ordinary tissue paper. To make paper chenille, glue rolled balls of tissue to selected areas. Rolling the balls is time consuming, so limit the decoration to small areas and use uncoated tissue because it will make smaller, more uniform balls.

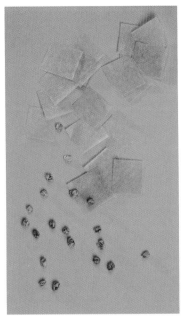

STEP 1

Cut tissue paper into 1" (2.5 cm) squares and roll them into small balls.

STEP 2

Working in small areas, apply white craft glue to the desired areas.

STEP 3

After filling in the area, let the glue dry.

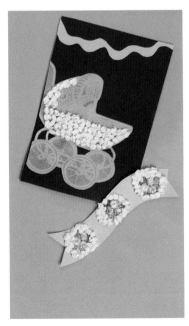

SAMPLES

Use the texture of chenille to highlight areas on print paper or to outline embroidered appliqués.

See the projects on pages 77, 79, and 86 that feature Chenille.

technique:
CROCHET

Homemakers of the '50s covered every armrest in the house with lacy handmade doilies. And that was just the beginning. Those who were proficient with a crochet hook could turn out coasters, place mats, tablecloths, and doll clothes in record time. Selected projects in this chapter sport only a hint of crochet with looped edging and premade mini doilies. Fortunately, to make this edging requires only one stitch, the chain stitch, which is easy to master. Follow the steps below to add flounce to flat paper.

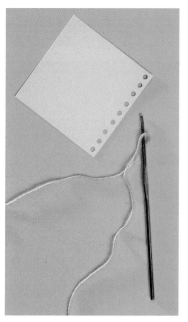

STEP 1

Punch holes in the edge of the paper. Make a slipknot in the floss and insert the end of the crochet hook in the loop.

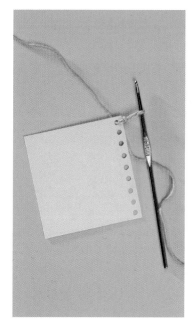

STEP 2

Working on the front side of the paper, insert the hook through the first hole and pull the floss through the hole and then through the loop.

STEP 3

Make five or six chain stitches and insert the hook through the second hole.

STEP 4

Complete the crochet stitches and knot the ends of the floss. Tape them to the back of the paper and trim the floss ends. Use premade mini doilies or lace if desired.

See the projects on pages 78 and 82 that feature Crochet.

Mini Projects

Ricrac Frame

Can an ordinary trim perk up a plain paper frame? Repeat rows of cotton and metallic ricrac to create a cheery picture.

1. Cut a frame from selected paper. Cut lengths of ricrac and place them on the frame. Apply contrasting paint over the ricrac in a random patter. Remove the ricrac and let the paint dry.
2. Cut varying lengths of ricrac and coat the backs with spray adhesive. Press them in place on the frame.
3. Trim the ricrac ends. Cut short lengths of ribbon and attach them to the frame with spray adhesive.

Button Wreath

Raid the button jar to make this charming ring.

1. Make a circle from medium-gauge wire.
2. Thread fine-gauge wire through the buttonholes, and wire the buttons to the circle.
3. Complete wiring the buttons to cover the circle, and use it to frame a photo or decorative paper coaster.

Blanket Frame

All wrapped up in cozy felt is the stuff sweet dreams are made of.

1. Buy prestitched felt in the gift-wrap section of your craft or department store. Or make your own by cutting felt into strips and stitching a blanket stitch along each edge.
2. Fold the strip at right angles to create mitered corners, and tack in place with matching thread.
3. Attach the folded strip to the page with double-sided adhesive and add embellishments.

LACE-UP REVIVAL

Remember lace-up books? Use long stitches again to describe outlines and to secure shapes.

1. Cut simple shapes from felt and place them on the paper.
2. Punch holes at the stitching points. Thread yarn through the holes to secure the shapes to the paper and knot the yarn on the back of the paper.
3. Cut around the shape and attach it to the front of a mini album.

TEDDY BEAR SPREAD

Today's the day this teddy bear is having a picnic. Choose a card with two layers of paper. (Refer to page 68 for Stenciling.)

1. Place the stencil on the fabric and, with a stencil brush or makeup sponge, apply the paint to the exposed area. Let dry.
2. With a craft knife, cut through the top layer of paper along selected lengths of the outline.
3. Add paper accents and die cuts and use a marker to add details to the face.

BRAIDED FRAME

Make a mixed-media frame with a twist: a braided and folded border. (Refer to page 71 for Braiding.)

1. Braid strips of pastel paper and fold them at right angles to match the window of the frame.
2. Add fuzzy coils and insert a paper tag or photo.

MINI PROJECTS

MACARONI GARDEN

It's all about the pasta inside this textured pastel garden. (Refer to page 69 for Macaroni Art.)

1. With a pencil, lightly draw the design on the background paper.
2. Apply thin layers of white craft glue to the marked areas and place colored macaroni in the wet glue.
3. Let the glue dry and add paper embellishments and a stamped title.

MANY MONOGRAMS COLLAGE

No identity crisis here.

1. Position and secure paper bits and the photo in a scattered arrangement.
2. Attach an assortment of monogram tags, tiles, and stickers to the page.

HERE, KITTY KITTY

The cat will definitely come back when honored on the front of this stylish fabric card.

1. Cut a strip of fabric that is shorter and wider than the print paper rectangle.
2. Place the stencil on the fabric and, with a stencil brush or makeup sponge, apply the paint to the exposed area. Let dry. (Refer to page 68 for Stenciling.)
3. Wrap the fabric around the rectangle and attach it to the card front. Add a paper accent.

FELT JACKET

Felt is a nonwoven material whose cut edges will not fray. This makes it perfect for fashioning mini clothing. Make this smart traveling jacket from three pieces: a large rectangle and two small rectangles.

1. Center and stitch the short sides of the small rectangles to the long sides of the large rectangle.
2. Cut a slit to the center and taper the neckline.
3. Add ric rac along the collar, then stitch up the sleeves and the sides to complete. Add a premade handbag with a safety pin. For more complex garments, use patterns for doll clothing.

IN THE LIME LIGHT

Add a textured border of paper chenille to a scalloped mat. (Refer to page 72 for Chenille.)

1. Layer and attach contrasting paper shapes and cut a round window through both layers.
2. With a pencil, lightly draw a larger circle around the window.
3. Cut ½" (1.3 cm) to ¾" (1.9 cm) squares from yellow tissue paper and roll them into compact balls. Glue the balls around the window with white craft glue and let dry. Tape the photo to the back, and add paper and brad accents.

CANDY NECKLACE FAT FRAME

Calling all candy lovers! Use your favorite edible accessory to make this sweet mat.

1. Cut a circle in a square of chipboard. Cut a larger circle in a square of Fome-cor.
2. Cover the Fome-cor with wrapping paper.
3. Cut a length of cord and thread candy rings on the cord.
4. Center and glue the covered Fome-cor to the chipboard. Use a hot-glue gun to glue the candy to the lip and sides of the round window. Knot and trim the cord ends and tape the photo to the back.

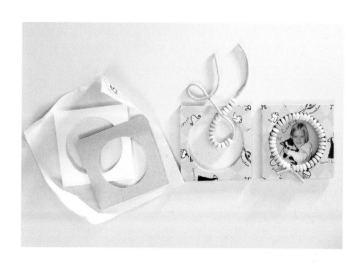

LAYOUTS

I'm Invited?

Come to our **P**arty

Tom & Angela Brown
June 28
bring a beach ball!

POOL PARTY

Be there or be square. Don't regret missing out on fun retro images and patterned papers.

THE DETAILS MAKE THE DIFFERENCE on this outdoor dinette set, from the space age boomerang pattern of the umbrella to the crocheted floss trim. The templates for the patio table, chairs, and umbrella are found on page 189. Cut the umbrella from the light pink paper and the boomerang shapes from the pink print. Attach the shapes to the umbrella and punch holes along the bottom edge. With a crochet hook, make a slipknot in the end of the floss and loop it through the first hole. Make six or seven chain stitches and then attach the strand through the next hole. Continue until the trim is complete. Tape the floss ends to the back of the umbrella. (Refer to page 73 for Crochet.) Cut the chairs from the light blue paper and the chair legs from the dark blue paper. Cut the tabletop from the cream print paper. Cut lengths of wire and bend them into shape. Arrange, and attach the chairs to the page. Tape the wire to the page. Cover the tape with the umbrella and the tabletop, and attach them to the page with the foam spacers. Cut a narrow strip from the zebra print and cut large sections from the stripe and geometric papers. Noting overlaps, arrange and attach the trimmed papers, photos, and beach ball on the page. Write a caption on the white paper and attach it to the top edge of the page with the tab sticker. Press the sticker in place and paint the title.

MATERIALS

- 12" x 12" (30.5 x 30.5 cm) pink herringbone paper for the background
- solid papers: white, pink, light green, dark green, and cream
- green print paper
- sunglasses novelty paper
- assorted paper tags
- pink tissue paper
- pink embroidery floss
- alphabet rub-ons
- computer printer
- pink acrylic paint

BLUSH

The number-one rule from a smart girl's guide to looking good—color everything pink!

USE SEVERAL SHADES OF PINK tissue to shade the flowers if desired. The templates for the flowers are found on page 190. Cut one large flower from pink paper. Cut 1" (2.5 cm) squares from the pink tissue paper and roll them into compact balls. (Refer to page 72 for Chenille.) Working in small areas, glue the balls on the template with white craft glue and let dry. Trace the small template on a tag, and glue chenille balls within the marked lines. Also glue chenille balls to the center of a flower on a preprinted tag. Thread lengths of embroidery floss through the tags and hang selected tags from a strip of green print paper. Cut or tear strips from the solid papers and cut a pair of sunglasses from the novelty paper. Noting overlaps, arrange and attach the strips, photos, and glasses to the page. Cut rectangles from the light green and cream paper and rub a letter on each for the title. Arrange and attach the title pieces, chenille flower, and remaining tag to the page. Print the caption on the white paper. Trim it and paint over the letters with diluted pink paint. After the paint dries, attach the caption box to the page.

MATERIALS

- 12" x 12" (30.5 x 30.5 cm) rust print paper for the background
- solid papers: brown, rust, cream, red, white, and purple
- plastic googly eyes
- plastic-coated green wire
- acrylic paints: black, tan, white, red, lavender, and blue
- rubber stamps: vintage toys and assorted alphabets
- black printing ink
- green slide frame
- cream button
- assorted alphabet stickers
- pink liquid poster paint
- liquid starch
- computer printer
- black fine-point marker

THE BEST THINGS IN LIFE

Remember when toys had springs and wheels instead of electronic bells and whistles?

A VARIETY OF TECHNIQUES are used to render classic toys, including stenciling, stamping, and paper piecing. Mix one part paint with one part starch. Drizzle the paint mixture on the purple paper and make swirls or other desired patterns with your fingers. Let the paint dry. If the paper is curled or bumpy, press it on the back with a hot iron. (Refer to page 70 for Finger Paint.) Tear a selected section from the painted paper. The stencil design for Mr. You-Know-Who is found on page 191. Cut a stencil for each color. (Refer to page 68 for Stenciling.) Place the body stencil on the cream paper, and use the tan paint to stencil the body. Let dry and stencil the remaining details with the designated colors. After the paint has dried, trim around the design. The template for the monkey is found on page 191. Cut the shapes from the designated colors, layer the smaller pieces, and attach them to the bodies. Use white craft glue to attach the googly eyes to the faces. Use the marker to draw the noses and mouths on the snouts. Cut a notched shape from the red paper. Print selected words of the title and trim around them. Noting overlaps, arrange and attach the painted paper, notched paper, photos, and monkeys to the page. Print the toys and arrange and attach the print words, potato head, slide frame, and button to the page. Shape the wire into eyeglasses and attach them to the page with paper-covered adhesive strips. Press the stickers in place and stamp the remaining words in the title. Use the marker to write the caption.

MATERIALS

- 12" x 12" (30.5 x 30.5 cm) brown print paper for the background
- solid papers: white, lavender, and cream
- taupe print paper
- silver tissue
- novelty papers: mouse, rabbit, rooster, and lion
- colored pencils
- preprinted title and text
- tea
- preprinted caption box
- dyed pasta: yellow and orange ancini di pepe and green spaghetti (Refer to page 69 for Macaroni Art)
- flower die cut
- yellow decorative ricrac

A LIST OF RHYMES

Two natty chickens and one well-worn rabbit make for good company in a nursery.

LOOK THROUGH SECONDHAND STORES to find old picture books with great text and illustrations. Cut or tear rectangles from the taupe print paper. Cut strips from the silver tissue and cream and lavender papers. Cut short lengths from the ricrac. Noting overlaps, arrange and attach the rectangles, strips, caption box, die cut, ricrac, and photos to the page. The templates for the chicks are found on page 190. (Refer to page 69 for Macaroni Art.) Draw them on the white paper, and using white craft glue, glue the pasta within the marked lines. Let dry. Cut around the shapes and attach them to the page. Cut the title and text into sections and dip selected sections in the tea to age them. (Refer to page 26 for Tea-Dyed Paper.) Let the sections dry and press with a hot iron if necessary. Tear the novelty papers into sections and color them with the pencils. Attach the title, text, and colored papers to the page.

MATERIALS

- 12" x 12" (30.5 x 30.5 cm) papers: taupe and taupe floral for the background
- solid papers: pink and white
- green print paper
- assorted paper scraps of coordinating prints and colors
- white vellum
- novelty papers: wood chips, nautical, script, and mini documents
- mini crocheted doilies
- assorted ribbons and trims
- jewel brads
- alphabet rubber stamps
- brown printing ink
- glass beads
- computer printer
- black fine-point marker

BY THE SEA

Do you long for the days of genuine romance? Stitch together a page that tells a tale of young love.

THE CROCHET ACCENTS are an important part of this composition and were purchased instead of stitched. Trim 1¼" (3.1 cm) from the side and bottom of the taupe floral paper and attach it to the taupe paper. Cut a small square from the pink paper and a large square from the vellum. Cut strips from the green print paper and stamp the title on one strip. Let dry. Place the squares and strips on the page and, with the sewing machine, stitch them to the page to secure. Pull the thread ends to the back of the page and tape them to secure. Trim the thread ends. Allowing 1½" (3.8 cm) on all sides, attach a selected photo to the pink paper. Cut lengths of ribbon, trim, and scrap papers and arrange them in a border around the photo. Machine stitch and/or glue them to the page to secure. Trim the pink paper to the edges of the ribbon. Insert the brads through the corners and secure the bordered photo to the page. Cut short lengths of ribbon trim and scrap paper. Cut small sections from the novelty papers. Arrange and attach the strips, novelty papers, doilies, and remaining photos to the page. Sprinkle the beads on the top corner and use small dots of white craft glue to secure them to the page. Print a caption on the white paper and trim around it. Slide it under the vellum edge to secure. Use the marker to write a caption on the photo.

MATERIALS

- 12" x 12" (30.5 x 30.5 cm) white paper for the background
- white paper
- brown paper scrap
- pink print paper
- assorted gold print fabrics
- gold velvet ribbon
- yellow print fabric
- poodle greeting card
- preprinted title box
- gray marker

LOOKING GOOD

The way it was and the way it is. Braid together a soft curtain of fabric to frame the moment.

CUT LARGE SECTIONS from the pink print paper and attach them to the white paper. Cut a rectangle from the yellow print fabric and cut caption boxes from the white and brown papers. Noting overlaps, arrange and attach the fabric rectangle, photos, card, title box, and caption boxes to the page. Cut the gold print fabrics into ¼" (6 mm) -wide strips. Secure the ends of three strips to the edge of the work surface and braid them together. (Refer to page 71 for Braiding.) Don't pull the fabric strands tightly when braiding, or the braids will buckle or curl. Use even tension to achieve flat and even braided strands. Repeat to make a total of five braided lengths. Cut a length of ribbon and notch the bottom end. Secure the braided lengths and ribbon to the page with strips of double-sided adhesive. Use the marker to write the caption.

TOAST AND JAM

The mundane never looked so good with this irreverent ode to toast.

SOME OF THE BEST PHOTOS and artwork around are found in vintage cookbooks. Buy one at a secondhand store and cut it up for borders and accents. Cut sections from the vellum and attach them to the melon paper. Cut a rectangle from the cream paper. Noting overlaps, arrange and attach the rectangle, photos, tag, and tiles to the page. The templates for the toast and the toaster are found on page 192. Cut a stencil for each color. (Refer to page 68 for Stenciling.) Place the toast on the foam and use the cream paint to stencil. Let dry. Stencil the remaining shapes and details for the crust and the toaster with the designated colors. Trim the foam and cookbook pages and attach them to the page.

MATERIALS

- 12" x 12" (30.5 x 30.5 cm) papers: brown print and taupe for the background

- solid papers: pink, orange, cream, and purple

- print papers: pink and blue

- dog die cut

- dyed pasta: yellow, orange, brown, and green ancini di pepe and green spaghetti (Refer to page 67 for Macaroni Art)

- preprinted title box

- white liquid poster paint

- liquid starch

- computer printer

BE KIND TO EVERYTHING THAT LIVES

Re-create the feel of a '50s picture book with this easy-to-make hot air balloon.

USE PASTA TO OUTLINE large shapes and define small ones. Tear the edge from the taupe paper and attach it to the brown print paper. The templates for the balloon and the grass are found on page 193. Cut the balloon sections from the pink and orange papers and attach them to the page. (Refer to page 142 for Paper Piecing.) Cut narrow strips from the pink print paper for the ropes. Layer and attach the dog and the ropes to the page. Using white craft glue and ancini di pepe, outline the sections of the balloon. Also use them to make the flower details. Draw the basket and the grass on the taupe paper. Glue the ancini di pepe within the marked lines

to make the basket and glue the spaghetti on the marked lines to make the grass. Let dry. Mix one part paint and one part starch. (Refer to page 70 for Finger Paint.) Drizzle the paint mixture on the corner of the page and swirl it around the balloon with your fingers. Also drizzle the paint mixture on the purple paper and swirl it. Let dry. Print the caption on the cream paper and cut it into two sections. Mount the caption sections on the purple paper and trim with cloud shapes topping the long section. Tear a strip from the blue print paper. Noting overlaps, arrange and attach the paper strip, photos, caption, and title box to the page.

MATERIALS

- 12" x 12" (30.5 x 30.5 cm) red pineapple print paper for the background
- solid papers: white and turquoise
- print papers: denim and diamond
- yellow tissue paper
- acrylic paint: orange, peach, white, gray, and black
- blue craft foam
- preprinted title strips
- question mark sticker
- black colored pencil

WHICH WAY TO THE BEACH?

Don't be confused by the direction of this page. Two diverse techniques merge to a successful end.

COPY THE LINE ART for the plane on a copy machine or draw it onto white paper with a black pencil. Or you can snip a photo of a plane from a magazine and add the chenille trim. The line art for the airplane is found on page 194. Cut ½" (1.3 cm) to ¾" (1.9 cm) squares from the yellow tissue paper and roll them into compact balls. (Refer to page 72 for Chenille.) Using white craft glue, glue the balls on the bottom of the plane and on the wing. Let dry. Cut or tear a rectangle from the turquoise paper. The template for the road is found on page 195. Cut the road from the denim paper and the wave shape from the diamond paper. Noting overlaps, arrange and attach the rectangle, plane, trimmed shapes, and photos on the page. The stencil design for the car is found on page 194. Cut a stencil for each color. (Refer to page 68 for Stenciling.) Place the body on the foam and use the orange paint to stencil the shape. Let dry. Stencil the remaining shapes and details in the designated colors. Trim a curved edge and narrow slit in the foam and attach it to the page. Cut a small strip stencil and stencil white lines on the road. Cut a narrow paper strip and attach it to the page with the title strips and sticker.

MATERIALS

- 12" x 12" (30.5 x 30.5 cm) text print paper
- assorted 12" x 12" (30.5 x 30.5 cm) two-toned print papers
- candy wrappers: gum and Pixy Stix
- preprinted title box
- letter die cuts
- sign language flash cards
- yellow lined paper
- black fine-point marker

FUN IN ANY LANGUAGE

Make this tactile border of bumpy braided paper and shiny wrappers.

FLASH CARDS MAKE GREAT page accents and they cover everything from former presidents to state capitals. Find them at the school supply store and start flashing. Arrange and attach the photos, flash cards, and candy wrappers to the page. Cut the two-toned paper into ¼" (6 mm) -wide strips. Secure the ends of three strips to the edge of the work surface and braid them together. (Refer to page 71 for Braiding.) Repeat to make two braided lengths. Arrange the braided strips with the Pixy Stix wrappers and tape them to the page to secure. Attach the title box and the die-cut letters to the page. Trim the yellow lined paper and attach it to the page. Use the marker to write the caption.

RETRO STYLE: THE '60S

THE DECADE OF THE 1960S was the inverted version of the month of March: It came in like a lamb and went out like a dancing and singing psychedelic lion. Suddenly, the post-war restrictions were gone and the baby boom generation shed the high mindedness and propriety they grew up with to become free thinkers and free spirits.

With traditional tastes turned upside down, especially in the art world, a red and white soup can became the symbol of good taste, and comic strips were enlarged and displayed on the walls of chic salons. Fashion, too, was revolutionized with the advent of a little eccentricity called the paper dress. Scott Paper Company surprised even itself when in 1966 they sold 500,000 of them. The dresses were designed to be throw-away whimsies, and were printed with lively paisley prints and graphic op-art designs. "After all," quipped one clothing designer, "who is going to do laundry in space?"

Carry this attitude over to scrapbook crafting and remember that almost anything goes. Use abstract lines and shapes, intense color, found-object artwork, and exaggerated scale. Also use repeated patterns of circles or stripes, or go '60s crazy and revive the boomerang shapes and atomic bursts of vintage Linoleum and Formica.

Love stamps, peace charms, and flower motifs are perfect embellishments for '60s-inspired layouts. To set an upbeat tone that is characteristic of the era, consider backgrounds of bright colors and graphic prints. Ethnic embroidery, quilted handcrafts, and tie-dyed T-shirts, all popular styles of the time, will add depth and authenticity to your pages. Iconic images such as the ubiquitous yellow smiley face bring a touch of whimsy.

technique:
CRAYON ART

Any school kid knows that melted crayons pack a punch. Why? When heat is applied to a colored area, the wax melts and distributes the pigments over the paper fibers. To maximize impact, use porous papers that will absorb the wax evenly. These include mulberry paper, rice paper, and newsprint.

STEP 1

Rub the ends of the crayons on a grater to make crumbs. Sprinkle the crumbs on the paper or draw solid shapes on the paper.

STEP 2

Sandwich the papers between sheets of typing paper and press with an iron.

STEP 3

Remove the blotting papers and let cool.

STEP 4

Trim the papers and attach them to the page.

See the projects on pages 106 and 109 that feature Crayon Art.

technique:
SAND PAINT

The unique texture of sand is both fuzzy and shiny. Because it is a natural material and can be dyed with bright colors, it was a hot design medium of the '60s. Artists were taken with it but because of its fluid nature, it was confined to decorative glass bottles and aquariums. Now with the availability of new adhesives, it is possible to evenly apply colored sand in both simple and detailed designs.

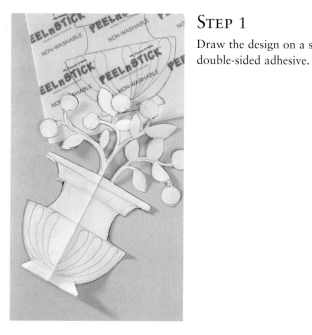

STEP 1

Draw the design on a sheet of double-sided adhesive.

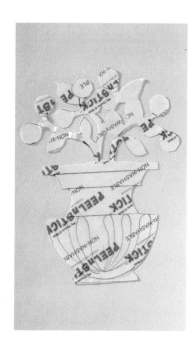

STEP 2

Cut around the outside shape of the design. Remove the backing paper and press the design in place on the page.

STEP 3

With a sharp craft knife, cut along the marked lines, through the top protective paper only. Remove the paper for the selected color. Sprinkle the colored sand on the exposed adhesive and remove the excess sand.

STEP 4

Repeat Step 3 for the remaining colors and add any desired accents.

See the projects on pages 100, 101, 105, 107, and 110 that feature Sand Paint.

technique:
STRING ART

A spiral string design mounted on a black velvet background ranks right up there with the velvet Elvis painting and the painting of dogs playing poker. However, the idea of adding simple string shapes as accents is a worthy one. This is easily achieved with the help of liquid starch and spray adhesive. Follow these simple steps to shape and mount the string.

STEP 1

Draw the design on the page and place a sheet of plastic over the design.

STEP 2

Dip the string on liquid starch.

STEP 3

Draw the string through pinched fingers to remove excess starch and shape it to match the marked design. Let dry.

STEP 4

Remove the dried shapes from the plastic. Coat the backs of the string shapes with spray adhesive and press them in place on the page.

See the projects on pages 107 and 109 that feature String Art.

technique:
EMBROIDERY

The Age of Aquarius was also the age of embroidered jeans and jackets, an age when a sprinkle of flowers on your shoulder or sleeve signaled enlightenment. You, too, can achieve a higher consciousness with only a needle and a skein of colored floss. Master these two easy stitches and create fetching shapes to highlight special pages.

STEP 1

Use an air-soluble marking pen to draw the design on the fabric.

STEP 2

Place the fabric between the rings of the embroidery hoop and tighten the hinge. Pull the fabric until it is taut.

STEP 3

Knot the end of the floss and bring it from the back to the front. Satin-stitch the design and add backstitching if desired. Knot the floss ends on the back of the fabric to secure.

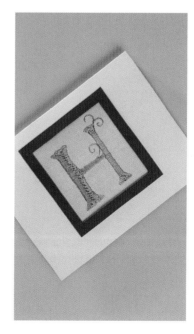

STEP 4

Press the fabric when the stitching is complete.

See the projects on pages 55 and 102 that feature Embroidery.

technique:
MACRAMÉ

An endless variety of knots can be used to make corded strips of geometric patterns. For example, knots alone were used to shape one of our favorite entries in the Crafters Hall of Fame, the macramé owl. OK, the owl may be out, but macramé is back, and in a big way. Noticed the mesh bags, belts, and jewelry on the pages of fashion magazines? You may be surprised to know that the knots and materials (minus the googly eyes) used to make fashion accessories today were used to make the owls. Use one simple knot to make many versions of serpentine macramé trim. It involves knotting outside strands around a center strand or a group of strands. Alter the look with beads or buttons.

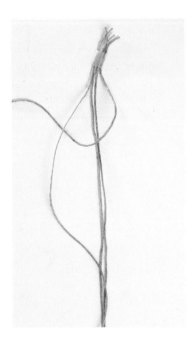

STEP 1

Cut four strands of twine and tape the ends to the work surface. Create a loop by placing the right strand over the two center strands and sliding it under the left strand.

STEP 2

Slide the left strand under the center strands and insert it through the loop to make a knot. Tighten the knot at the tops of the strands.

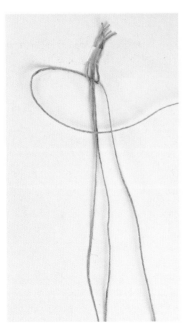

STEP 3

Create a loop by placing the left strand over the two center strands and sliding it under the right strand.

STEP 4

Slide the right strand under the center strands and insert it through the loop to make a second knot. Tighten the knot. Repeat this process of alternating the right strand under the left and the left under the right to make a knotted strand.

See the projects on pages 100, 103, and 111 that feature Macramé.

technique:
PATCHWORK

A saucy fabric stew, patchwork was served up as clothing and linens for much of the sweet and swinging '60s. Piece some together to display your favorite snippets of history. Begin by selecting the perfect combination of papers. For a subtle composition, use papers of the same color family and value range. For drama, use a variety of hues, patterns, and values.

STEP 1

Draw a grid of 1" (2.5 cm) squares on the paper. Cut selected papers into squares. The papers for the sample are cut into 4" (10.2 cm) squares.

STEP 2

Coat the backs of the paper squares with spray adhesive. Using the marked lines as guides, press the squares in place on the page.

STEP 3

Offset and overlap selected squares to create an uneven pattern.

STEP 4

Press the squares in place to cover the remaining grid.

See the projects on pages 98, 108, and 111 that feature Patchwork.

Painted Rocks

Rock your world with these bright painted pebbles. (Refer to page 146 for Clay Art.)

1. Shape air-drying modeling clay into rock shapes. Make them slightly raised, with flat backs for easy attachment. Let dry.
2. Sand the edges if desired.
3. Coat the clay rocks with acrylic paint.
4. Paint the details on the coated rocks and let dry.

Patchwork and Potted Plants

Patchwork wallpaper shows off an inviting collection of pots. (Refer to page 97 for Patchwork.)

1. Use a straight-edge ruler and craft knife to cut the patterned rectangles.
2. Coat the backs with spray adhesive and press them in place with abutting edges.
3. Add die-cut pots and flowers and a textured linen border.

Paisley Frame

Be passionate about paisley with an embossed clay frame. (Refer to page 146 for Clay Art.)

1. Roll out air-drying clay on the work surface. Cut a frame shape from the clay.
2. Press paisley stamps in the moist clay.
3. Let dry and sand the edges with fine sandpaper. Coat the frame with lavender acrylic paint. Let the paint dry and sand the surface lightly to highlight the impressed images.

SHIFTING STRIPES

Coming to a journal near you: offset stripes and dancing charms.

1. Line up paper strips with abutting edges. Center and stamp the image.
2. Realign the strips with irregular top and bottom edges. Punch holes along the top and bottom edges.
3. Thread metallic ribbon through the top holes and thread gold charms through the bottom holes. Secure the ribbon ends and thread ends to the back of the paper.

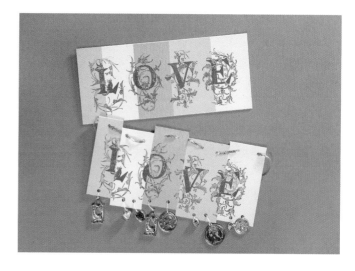

DROP SHADOW LETTERS

Get your groove on with block letters and swinging color combinations.

1. Cut two sets of letters from contrasting papers.
2. Attach one set to the paper using glue dots or spray adhesive. Offset the second set of letters, with the first set serving as shadows. Attach the second set with adhesive foam spacers.

TIE-DYE T-SHIRT

What? No clumsy string and messy dye? This fun and easy method will fit you to a tee.

1. Cut a section of fabric from a white T-shirt. Draw rows of circles or stripes on the fabric with water-based markers.
2. With a squirt bottle, lightly soak the fabric with rubbing alcohol. Let dry.
3. Cut a T-shirt shape from the fabric and stitch the hem and sleeve seams with contrasting thread. Attach the T-shirt to paper with spray adhesive and add accents.

SOUP MAT

Pay homage to Andy Warhol and mass marketing with a snappy red mat.

1. Carefully remove the labels from Campbell's soup cans.
2. Coat the backs of the labels with spray adhesive and press them in place on a paper mat. Trim the labels to fit with a straight-edge ruler and craft knife.
3. Cut rectangles from red cellophane and attach them to the corners of the mat with strips of double-sided adhesive.

MACRAMÉ FRAME

Reviving the art of the knot. (Refer to page 96 for Macramé.)

1. Begin with a 2¾" (7 cm) (or larger) metal ring. Cut eight 6" (15.2 cm) lengths of hemp twine and loop each around the ring.
2. Snugly wrap the twine around the entire ring with the loops evenly spaced. Knot one end of each loop with alternating ends and trim the ends.
3. Attach a floss tassel and a flower-shaped button on the bottom of the ring. Attach frame over a photo already attached to the page.

SPLASHY SAND MAT

Make it real and make it sandy with this playful grainy border. Choose a background paper with a bold pattern that will show through the translucent sand. (Refer to page 93 for Sand Paint.)

1. Draw a border design on the paper side of a sheet of double-sided adhesive.
2. Cut around the outside edge, remove the backing, and press in place. Cut through the protective paper, along the marked interior lines.
3. According to color, remove the first set of protective paper sections and sprinkle the selected color on the exposed adhesive. Remove the excess sand and repeat for the remaining colors.

FAUVE ORNAMENT

The '60s marked the rebirth of fauvism, a style of art from the early 1900s when vivid colors ruled supreme. (Refer to page 93 for Sand Paint.)

1. Choose an ornament with hollow spaces. Place the ornament on the paper and trace the areas that will receive the sand and decorative motifs.
2. Transfer the shapes to the paper side of a sheet of double-sided adhesive. Cut out the shapes, remove the backing, and press in place on the paper.
3. According to color, remove the protective paper and sprinkle the sand on the exposed adhesive. Remove the excess sand and repeat for the remaining colors.
4. Attach the ornament to the page with narrow strips of double-sided adhesive.

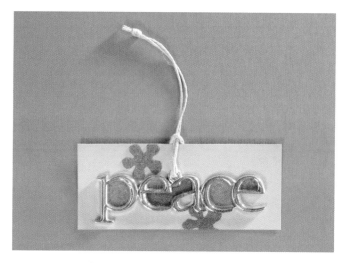

CREEPY CRAWLERS

What's in store for wandering bugs? A permanent home on a paint-splattered page. (Refer to page 117 for Paint Art.)

1. Drip acrylic paint onto the paper.
2. While the paint is wet, press the plastic bugs into the paint. Let dry and add the caption. Add more paint drops if desired.

STOP STENCIL

Stop traffic with this bold stenciled sign. (Refer to page 68 for Stenciled Paper.)

1. Select the stencil letters.
2. Hold the edges of the stencil while applying the paint. Let each letter dry before stenciling the next.
3. Complete the word or phrase and add a photo, a paper cutout, and rub-on letters.

MATERIALS

- 12" x 12" (30.5 x 30.5 cm) palm tree print blue paper
- solid papers: light blue, light green, and turquoise
- vellum: white and green
- silver tissue paper
- blue cotton knit fabric
- green embroidery floss
- alphabet rub-ons
- paper monogram coaster
- black fine-point marker

BLUE HAWAII

Cool colors and bumpy titles lend to the dreamlike quality of well-spent days.

AN OLD T-SHIRT was used as the backing for the embroidered palm trees. Use old clothes if they have sentimental value or are made from interesting fabrics. Cut the solid papers and the green vellum into squares, rectangles, and strips. Tear a strip of tissue paper and trim the top from the coaster. Noting overlaps, arrange and attach the paper shapes, coaster, and photos to the page. Rub the letters onto the photo and use the marker to write the short caption.

The template for the palm tree is found on page 196. Allowing at least 2" (5.1 cm) around each, transfer two trees to the fabric with an air-soluble marking pen. Satin-stitch within the marked areas. (Refer to page 95 for Embroidery.) Trim around the stitched trees and press them if necessary. Coat the backs of the fabric rectangles with spray adhesive and attach them to the page. Cut a strip of white vellum and attach it to the page. Use the marker to write a second caption.

MATERIALS

- 12" x 12" (30.5 x 30.5 cm) blue print paper for the background
- solid papers: taupe, pink, blue, green, and turquoise
- stitched stripes print paper
- hemp twine
- assorted beads
- assorted buttons
- alphabet stickers
- preprinted message strip
- caption strip
- blue felt
- blue brads

MACRAMANIA

Strut your knotted stuff with macramé strands placed side by side on a page.

THIS PAGE FEATURES a collection of knotted strands. All but one are a variation of the basic macramé knot. Cut rectangles from the taupe and the stripe print paper. Arrange and attach the rectangles and photos to the page. From left to right, the first row is made with two hemp strands in the center and one on each side. Knot the outside strands over the inside strands and thread yellow beads along one edge at ¾" (1.9 cm) increments. The second row is not made with knots. It is made with buttons and beads that are threaded onto four strands of hemp in a random pattern. The third, fourth, and fifth rows are variations of the first row. The fifth row is made by looping short strands of hemp around a paper strip and trimming the edges. (Refer to page 96 for Macramé.) Make these or other variations, and attach the strands to the page with narrow strips of double-sided adhesive or short paper-covered strips. Attach the message strips and short caption strips to the page. Cut felt circles and use the brads to secure them to the page. Make hemp tassels and tie them to the brads.

MATERIALS

- 12" x 12" (30.5 x 30.5 cm) cream print paper for the background
- solid papers: white and melon
- watercolor paints: green and yellow
- print papers: cream floral and pink petal
- green vellum
- cream mulberry tissue
- pressed flowers (Refer to page 22 for Pressed Flowers)
- embroidered flower appliqués
- assorted leaf rubber stamps
- green printing ink
- leaf punch
- computer printer
- green colored pencil

FLOWER SHOWERS

Mix and match stitched and dried flowers for a combination that can't be beat.

THE STITCHED FLOWERS on this page came from a throw-away throw pillow. Scour thrift stores for pillows or dresser scarves that have salvageable stitching. Cut a large square from the cream print paper and a small square from the pink print paper. Also cut strips from the melon paper and the vellum. Punch sections of the vellum strips with the leaf punch. Noting overlaps, arrange and attach the squares, strips, and photos to the page. Stamp leaf shapes on the page.

From the mulberry tissue, tear shapes that are slightly larger than the flowers. Layer and attach the torn shapes and the appliqués to the page. Coat the backs of the pressed flowers and leaves with spray adhesive and carefully press them to the page. Print the title on the white paper and cut around the individual letters. Paint them with the watercolor paints and let dry. Attach them to the page. Use the colored pencil to write the captions.

MATERIALS

- 12" x 12" (30.5 x 30.5 cm) pink paper for the background
- solid papers: light blue and turquoise
- print papers: pink polka dot and cream plaid
- colored sand: blue, green, yellow, pink, and black
- fabric appliqué
- blue marker
- black colored pencil
- die-cut alphabet letters

LOVE THE EARTH

Nothing new under the sun? How about your favorite planet rendered in bright sand?

SAND IS ABRASIVE, so cover this page with a clear sleeve to prevent it from damaging facing photos. The template for the Earth is found on page 196. (Refer to page 93 for Sand Paint.) Draw the design on the paper side of a double-sided adhesive sheet. Cut around the outside edges, remove the backing paper, and press the shapes in place on the light blue paper. Cut through the protective paper, along the marked interior lines. Remove the protective paper from the sea shapes and sprinkle blue sand on the exposed adhesive.

Remove the excess sand and repeat for the remaining shapes and colors. Trim the edges of the blue paper. Cut large sections from the plaid paper and cut strips with a scalloped edge from the polka-dot paper. Cut a rectangle from the turquoise paper. Cut a notched shape from the light blue paper. Noting overlaps, arrange and attach the paper shapes, letters, sand painting, photos, and the appliqué to the page. Use the marker to complete the title, and use the pencil to write the captions.

MATERIALS

- 12" x 12" (30.5 x 30.5 cm) lavender paper for the background
- solid papers: green, white, and purple
- dot paper
- ink blot novelty paper
- yellow mulberry tissue paper
- crayons: yellow, peach, and green
- computer printer

Zachary defies the laws of gravity and the laws of nature. He is able to eat drink and sleep on a skate board.

GRATER SKATER

For a high-flying op-art backdrop, lose the coloring books but keep the crayons.

COVER YOUR IRONING BOARD with newspaper or scrap paper to prevent the wax from marking the board. Place a large section of tissue on blotting paper. Grate the crayons and sprinkle the crumbs on the tissue paper. (Refer to page 92 for Crayon Art.) Cover the paper and wax crumbs with more paper and press. Trim the tissue if necessary and cut or tear rectangles and strips from the green and novelty papers. Noting overlaps, arrange and attach the trimmed papers, tissue paper, and photos to the page. Print the title on the white paper and trim around it. Attach the title box and a strip of purple paper on the page.

MATERIALS

- 12" x 12" (30.5 x 30.5 cm) rust print paper for the background
- solid papers: yellow and white
- watercolor paints: orange and pink
- gold floral print paper
- print vellum
- novelty papers: cherries, flower, nest, and butterfly
- gauze
- ivory sand
- clear acrylic strip
- string
- liquid starch
- computer printer

GUARDIAN ANGEL

Translucent vellum gives this string angel a "through the looking glass" quality.

MAKE THE STRING SHAPES ahead of time, as they require several hours to dry. Cut irregular shapes from the gauze and attach them to the page with spray adhesive. Cut a smaller shape from a double-sided adhesive sheet. Remove the backing paper and press in place on the gauze. Remove the protective paper and sprinkle the sand on the exposed adhesive. (Refer to page 93 for Sand Paint.) The templates for the angel, script, and star are found on pages 197 and 198. Cut out the head and carefully tear the angel body from the vellum. Place the angel on the work surface and cover it with a sheet of clear plastic. Cut a length of string and dip it into liquid starch. (Refer to page 94 for String Art.) Shape it into loops that echo the shape of the angel. Repeat the process for the

words. Coat the backs of the string shapes with spray adhesive and press them in place on the page. Cut stars from the yellow paper and attach them to the page. Attach the head to the page with a matching shape of double-sided adhesive and attach the body with paper-covered adhesive strips. Cut irregular shapes from the floral paper and attach the paper shapes and photo to the page. Cut shapes from the novelty papers and place them on the edge of the photo. Attach a strip of double-sided adhesive to the back of the acrylic strip. Center the adhesive on the shapes and secure to the page. Print the title and caption on the white paper and cut it into separate strips. Paint them with the watercolor paints and let dry. Attach the strips and the butterfly to the page.

Santa Monica
California

wild ride

thrills

amusement park

favorite moments
Zack- the star fish
Garret- roller blades
Keaton- double-
ice cream cones

MATERIALS

- 12" x 12" (30.5 x 30.5 cm) white polka dot and pink papers for the background
- white paper
- dot paper
- coordinating papers for patchwork
- flower border
- mini paper embellishments: ferris wheel, roller coaster cart, and message tags
- computer printer

PIER GROUP

A ground of patchwork is the perfect metaphor for a family: individual parts joined together by love.

BECAUSE THE BACKGROUND page and the patchwork pieces are all square, the patchwork layout is turned "on point" to add interest. Trim the bottom and sides from the pink paper and attach it to the white polka dot paper. With a pencil and a ruler, lightly draw diagonal grid lines on the bottom of the pink paper to form 2" (5.1 cm) squares. Cut 2" (5.1 cm) squares, a few 1" (2.5 cm) squares, and a few 1" x 2" (2.5 x 5.1 cm) rectangles from the coordinating papers. Attach the squares and rectangles to the page within the marked lines, and trim the edges. (Refer to page 97 for Patchwork.) Cut strips from the dot paper. Attach the strips, flower border, photo, and paper embellishments to the page. Attach the message tags with paper-covered adhesive strips. Print the title and caption on the white paper. Trim around them and attach to the page.

MATERIALS

- 12" x 12" (30.5 x 30.5 cm) pink paper for the background
- mulberry tissue paper: pink and blue
- white tissue paper
- acrylic paint: lavender and pink
- pink paper
- assorted accent paper scraps
- purple pearl cotton floss
- crayons
- black colored pencil
- computer printer

AMERICAN GRAFFITI

Picture this—girl power illustrated with crayons and string.

COVER YOUR IRONING BOARD with newspaper or scrap paper to prevent the wax from marking the board. Make the string shapes ahead of time because they require several hours of drying time. Draw bold images on large sections of tissue paper. Sandwich the artwork between blotter paper and press. (Refer to page 92 for Crayon Art.) Tear the edges of the papers. Cut snippets from the accent papers. Noting overlaps, arrange and attach the tissue sections, accent papers, and photo to the page. Place a sheet of plastic on the work surface. Cut a length of pearl cotton and dip it into liquid starch.

(Refer to page 94 for String Art.) Shape it into a loose coil or a flower. Repeat to make additional coils and/or flowers. Let dry and trim the ends if necessary. Coat the backs of the string shapes with spray adhesive and press them in place on the page. The template for the title is found on page 199. Cut a stencil for the title. (Refer to page 68 for Stenciling.) Place the stencil on the white tissue paper and fill with pink and lavender paints. Let dry and trim. Draw accent lines in selected areas with the black pencil. Print the caption on the pink paper and trim. Attach the title and the caption to the page.

wisdom begins in wonder.

MATERIALS

- 12" x 12" (30.5 x 30.5 cm) white paper for the background
- solid papers: blue, black, and turquoise
- vellum: spatter and text
- colored sand: orange, tan, mint, pink, and blue

PAINTED DESERT

Dust on the color and soon you will be looking at a horizon of sand and sky.

CUT SECTIONS FROM the blue paper and the spatter vellum and attach them to the page. The template for the title is found on page 200. Cut the title from the text vellum and, noting overlaps, attach the title and the photos to the page. Cut an 11" x 4½" (27.9 x 11.4 cm) rectangle from the turquoise paper. The template for the desert border is found on page 200. (Refer to page 93 for Sand Paint.) Draw the design on the paper side of a double-sided adhesive sheet. Cut around the outside edges, remove the backing paper, and press the shape in place on the turquoise rectangle. Cut through the protective paper, along the marked interior lines. Remove the orange sections and sprinkle the sand on the exposed adhesive. Remove the excess sand and repeat for the remaining shapes and colors. Trim around the top edge of the design and save the top right corner of the border. Attach the sand design and the corner to the page. Cut irregular strips from the black paper and attach the strips and the caption box to the page.

MATERIALS

- 12" x 12" (30.5 x 30.5 cm) melon paper for the background
- solid papers: mint and black
- coordinating papers for patchwork
- antique postcards
- paper twist handle (from a gift bag)
- green silk ribbon
- alphabet stencils
- mint gauze
- red rayon thread
- ivory fish
- acrylic paint: black and white

PRINCE OF TIDES

Patchwork diamonds carry the day for an evocative travel page. Macramé and 3-D accents complete the mood.

SOFT GAUZE MAKES perfect nautical netting. If the gauze you purchase is slightly stiff, launder it to remove any sizing. With a pencil and a ruler, lightly draw diagonal grid lines on the melon paper to form diamond shapes that measure 1½" x 3¾" (3.8 x 9.5 cm). (Refer to page 97 for Patchwork.) Cut matching diamonds from the coordinating papers. Attach them in a random pattern to the page within the marked lines and trim the edges. Tear strips from the mint paper. Noting overlaps, arrange and attach the postcards, torn strips, and photos to the page. Cut two lengths of ribbon and tape the ends of the ribbon and the top of the paper twist handle to the work surface. With the handle in the center, knot the ribbon lengths over the paper twist. (Refer to page 96 for Macramé.) Tie knots in the ribbon ends to secure. Use the black paint to stencil the title to the page. (Refer to page 68 for Stenciling.) Paint the first two words of the title on a strip of black paper and let dry. Attach a section of gauze, the knotted handle, and the title strip to the page. Thread the fish and hang them from the handle or top edge of the page.

road trip

HIGHER EDUCATION

Mary and Ivy love the campus and their new apartment. It's the studying that they are not so crazy about.

ought a new meaning to "Shop 'til you Drop".

CARNIVAL

RETRO STYLE: THE '70S

DIG UP YOUR *Charlie's Angels* T-shirt because the '70s are back and better than ever. This was a decade of contrasts, both more refined and more ridiculous than the '60s. People became bored with civil disobedience as a hobby and took up disco dancing instead. They started washing their hair again, only to curl it into lion manes. (And that was just the men.) Gas lines, leisure suits, and pet rocks ... could it get any crazier?

Popular culture was definitely reflected in design styles. Anything that announced your love for the Earth (the first Earth Day was proclaimed in 1970) was hot. We ate natural foods and vowed not to litter. Wallpaper, fabric, and even stationery were all covered with trees and sunsets. But a kind of romantic bohemian look was also popular. Stained glass, wrought iron, and velvet lent an air of drama and mystery to clothing and home decorating accents. Keep three prototypes in mind: the disco dancer, the granola lover, or the long-haired poet and design your pages accordingly.

Use pure hues or dark jewel-toned colors of green and purple. Glitter, velvet, and frayed denim are good texture choices, and you can't go wrong with geometric shapes. Also incorporate themes of flowers, castles, and Edwardian collars and cuffs.

Take a backseat to no one when it comes to '70s cultural awareness, and remember to keep on truckin'.

What is hot one decade often becomes the nightmare of the next. This was especially true of the 1970s, and it took thirty years for us to once again appreciate the outrageousness of these bad fads. The revived style includes trimmed paper or craft foam to add flat areas of color, and shiny accents of glitter and embossing grains. Subtle is definitely not the approach to surface decoration of '70s style, so go bold with both background paper and accents. For added texture, you can't go wrong with fake fur and denim.

technique:
DISTRESSED DENIM

The '70s will long be known as the decade of "jeans as canvas," meaning that denim jeans were used for clothing and artistic expression (not necessarily in that order). This trend started in the '60s and continues today, but it was most pronounced during the days of gas lines and fondue parties. The distinctive color and weave of denim makes it a great accent for paper, and it can be bleached, frayed, and painted.

STEP 1
Crinkle a swatch of denim and dip it in bleach.

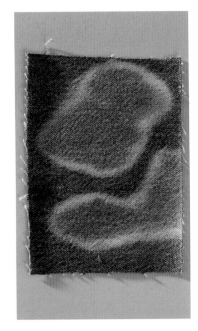

STEP 2
Remove the swatch and rinse it thoroughly with cold water. Let dry.

STEP 3
To fray the outside edges, remove the exposed threads. To fray a section within the swatch, cut two parallel slits horizontally in the denim. Loosen the threads along the cut edges and, working from the center out, pull the vertical threads to remove them.

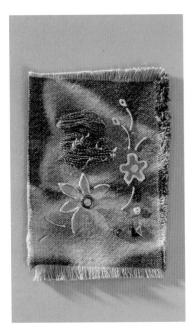

STEP 4
Add acrylic paint, dimensional paint, studs, or buttons as desired.

See the projects on pages 129 and 132 that feature Distressed Denim.

technique:
PAINT ART

Think "explosion" on the paint aisle. Everything from beach towels to billboards was decorated with energetic bursts of color. In the spirit of the times, try these paint techniques, which are deliberate but retain the spontaneous nature of splashed or dripped paint.

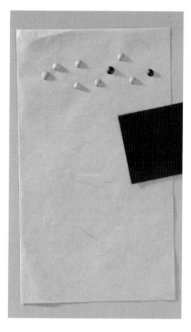

STEP 1 FOR PULLED PAINT

For pulled designs, drop acrylic paint beads along the top of the paper.

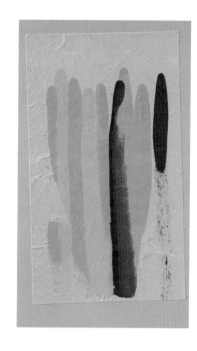

STEP 2 FOR PULLED PAINT

Using a small piece of chipboard for a squeegee, vertically pull the paint on the page. Let dry.

STEP 1 FOR DRIPPED PAINT

For drip designs, drop acrylic paint beads at random spots on the page. Also draw wavy lines with the dimensional paint.

STEP 2 FOR DRIPPED PAINT

Overlapping the beads and the lines, place foam cutouts on the page. Let dry, and add more paint lines and drops if desired.

See the projects on pages 101, 122, 124, 128, and 133 that feature Paint Art.

technique:
VEGETABLE PRINTS

Vegetable prints are found at the intersection of artistic expression and good nutrition. A trend that started in elementary schools and made its way to exclusive galleries, printing with natural objects is easy and fun. There is enough natural dye in red cabbage to color the paper without requiring additional paint or ink. Also, the folds of the cabbage leaves make a beautiful marbled design. Other vegetables to consider are those with an interesting cross section such as green peppers and jalapeño peppers.

STEP 1 FOR CABBAGE PRINTS

For cabbage prints, use a large knife to cut chunks with flat sides from the cabbage.

STEP 2 FOR CABBAGE PRINTS

Press the cut sides on the page.

STEP 1 FOR PEPPER PRINTS

For pepper prints, cut a cross section of the pepper.

STEP 2 FOR PEPPER PRINTS

Dip the cut sides in paint or ink and press them in place on the page.

See the projects on pages 130 and 137 that feature Vegetable Prints.

technique:
STAINED GLASS

Actual stained glass is made by cutting colored glass into shapes and then fitting all the pieces together with lead channel. Here, cut paper overlays serve as the leading network and paint, paper, and embossing grains substitute for the glass. Use a craft knife with a sharp point to make clean cuts in the corners and curves of the overlay paper.

STEP 1

Use a sheet of typing paper to make a template. Tape the template to the dark paper and cut out the shapes with a craft knife to make the "lead." Also cut around the outside edge.

STEP 2

Remove the template from the paper.

STEP 3

Place the template on the light paper and trace around the inside shapes. Fill in the shapes with paper and paint. Note that large shapes can be used when the neighboring sections are the same color. Let dry.

STEP 4

Coat the back of the lead layer with spray adhesive. Align the lead layer to cover the divisions and press in place on the page.

See the projects on pages 126 and 135 that feature Stained Glass.

technique:
GLITTER ART

Become one of the glitterati by sporting glitzy flakes that reflect the spirit of the times. Glitter comes in fine or chunky flakes and is designed to reflect light and add texture. Dress up your paper projects with any or all of the techniques described.

TECHNIQUE 1

Cut strips from double-sided adhesive and remove the paper backing. Press the strips on the paper. Remove the protective paper and sprinkle glitter on the exposed adhesive. Remove the excess glitter.

TECHNIQUE 2

Dilute acrylic paint to one part paint and one part water and mix glitter into the paint. Paint the paper with the paint and glitter mixture.

TECHNIQUE 3

Dilute white craft glue to one part glue and two parts water. Paint the glue on the edges of the paper and on any additional areas. Quickly sprinkle fine glitter on the wet glue, and remove the excess glitter. Let dry.

TECHNIQUE 4

Coat the front of the paper with spray adhesive. Sprinkle large flake glitter on the adhesive and remove the excess glitter. Sprinkle fine glitter in a contrasting color on the adhesive, and remove the excess glitter.

See the projects on pages 124, 127, and 136 that feature Glitter.

technique:
EMBOSSED VELVET

How did we get so cool in the '70s? Big hair, big collars, and big sleeves, with two of the three made from fuzzy crushed velvet. Velvet clothing in dark jewel-tone colors was all the rage and so were fuzzy velvet posters. To make embossed designs in velvet, choose a fabric with a rayon blend. Also choose stamps with simple graphic designs. If you are using a foam stamp, make sure it is made from dense foam that won't melt when exposed to heat. Rubber stamps and wood shapes also can be used to make the impressions.

STEP 1

Choose a stamp.

STEP 2

Place the stamp right side up on the work surface. With the wrong side up, cover the stamp with the velvet. Set the iron on cotton and mist the wrong side of the velvet with water. Hold the iron steady on the stamp for five to ten seconds.

STEP 3

Let the fabric dry. Don't apply additional heat to the design area.

FUZZY POSTERS

For a similar look, add sections of fuzzy posters to your pages. Posters are sold with markers for coloring. For an alternative, try stamping the exposed areas with stamping inks to color.

See the projects on pages 131 and 134 that feature Embossed Velvet.

MINI PROJECTS

PAINTED FRAME

On your way to a Village People concert and don't have time for needlework? Try liquid stitching, an easy way to add a floating, embroidered decoration to almost any surface.

1. Combine fabric and paper to make a frame. (Refer to page 117 for Paint Art.)
2. Add paper accents and draw capricious lines of paint around the outside border.

PLATFORM SHOE

Take yourself to Funky Town in this leather platform complete with goldfish. Real suede contrasts with faux Plexiglas for a quirky paper illustration.

1. Layer the shapes in the following order: the shadow (cut from coordinating paper), platform soul, goldfish, clear cellophane, and inside shoe.
2. Attach the two leather pieces to complete the shoe.
3. Finish with dimensional paint stitches.

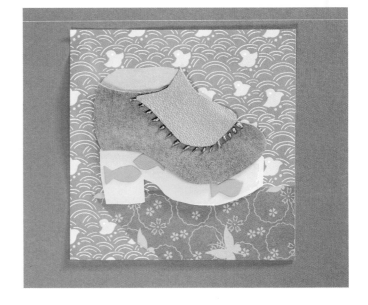

SPATTER APPLIQUÉ

Scrap art that featured appliqué and embroidery once graced everything from bell-bottoms to backpacks to baby blankets. Get the same funky look in a fraction of the time with spray adhesive and dimensional paint. (Refer to page 117 for Paint Art.)

1. Cut the shapes from selected fabrics.
2. Secure them to the paper with spray adhesive. (When using fabric as a backdrop, use fabric adhesive or fusible web to secure the shapes to the fabric.)
3. Write a message and add shading dots with dimensional paint.

Fair Hat for Foul Weather

Make a dreamy hat by reshaping a soft baby sock.

1. Cut the top from the sock at a slight angle and roll the cut edge to create a cuff.
2. Stitch a crocheted doily on the front to decorate. (Refer to page 71 for Crochet.) Add fuzzy or furry accessories to display.

Ojo de Dios

Back in the day, these ethnic curiosities were made from twigs and yarn and were spotted hanging from the rearview mirrors of Pintos and Volkswagen Beetles. "Ojo de Dios" is Spanish for "Eye of God," with the center of the weaving representing a benevolent and watchful eye. This version has been flattened to accommodate album pages by using paper and pearl cotton floss.

1. Make three 3" (7.6 cm) strips from stiff paper. Layer a horizontal strip between two vertical strips to make a cross and glue in place.
2. Begin wrapping with diagonal threads. Working in a counterclockwise direction, wrap across the center on the front of the cross, around the spoke, and back to the front. Rotate ninety degrees and repeat. Change the floss colors as desired.
3. Leave the paper ends exposed and secure the loose ends of the floss to the back of the paper.

Paper Chain

Play "Connect-the-Die Cuts" with this eye-catching chain made from fat links of paper.

1. Cut paper squares, ¾" (1.9 cm) or larger, from print paper.
2. Cut through one side of the square and cut a circle in the center. Trim the corners to change the squares to octagons. Connect the links to each other at the slits. Tape the slits closed on the back of the paper with small strips of cellophane tape.
3. Use decorative ribbon to tie the ends to the page.

STAR MAT

Forget stars that twinkle and go for those that burst into color.

1. Using a scrap of chipboard as a squeegee, evenly spread thick poster paint on the paper. (Refer to page 117 for Paint Art.)
2. While the paint is wet, dribble individual drops of contrasting acrylic paint onto the paint.
3. With a straight pin, guide the paint from the center out to make star shapes.

AZURE SKY SUN CATCHER

A cure for the anytime blues.

1. Color a sunny face on the etched side of shrink plastic. Note that the plastic will shrink to fifty percent of its original size. Bake according to the manufacturer's directions.
2. Cut a free-swinging halo of rays from trimmed paper and cover it with blue glitter. (Refer to page 120 for Glitter Art.) Hang it from a window corner or tape it to a mini foam plaque.

DISCO FAT FRAME

The universal symbol of the '70s, the disco ball, is the inspiration for a mini-mirrored frame.

1. Cover a small square of Fome-cor with soft and stretchy plush.
2. Use a glue gun to attach mirror tiles, paper tiles, and plastic gems.

PLASTIC FANTASTIC GUITAR

Break on through to the other side with a novelty guitar and rowdy, mismatched papers. To achieve a three-dimensional look, plant the guitar in a hollowed-out scrap of Fome-cor.

1. Cover the Fome-cor with polka dot paper. Trace the shape of the guitar with a pencil or marker. Cut through all the layers with a craft knife.
2. Cut a larger outline of the guitar from the contrasting paper and snip short, perpendicular slits around the outside edge. Choose a paper that is lightweight enough to be pliant.
3. Wrap the guitar in the paper and press in place. Glue the paper to the covered Fome-cor and the guitar to the paper. Add the embellishments.

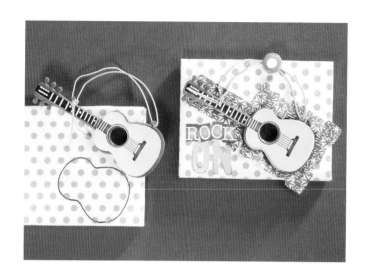

GLASS FLOWERS

Foil a boring page with a flower triptych. By adding copper leaf trim to the edges, they mimic stained glass windows.

1. Stamp and color flowers on the etched side of shrink plastic rectangles. Note that the plastic will shrink to fifty percent of its original size. Bake according to the manufacturer's directions.
2. Attach thin strips of double-sided adhesive to the edges. Remove the protective paper and place the copper leaf on the exposed adhesive. Use a soft brush to flatten and remove excess copper leaf.

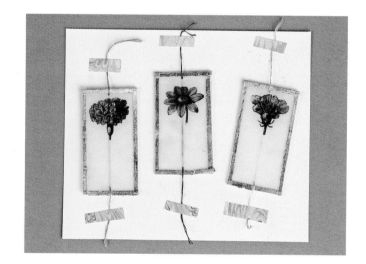

FAUX TILE FRAME

Simulate the far-out look of broken tile mosaics with polymer clay and stickers. (Refer to page 146 for Clay Art.)

1. Knead the clay and roll it to approximately ⅜" (1 cm) thick.
2. Cut a rectangle and a centered window. Using a tool with a flattened tip, make indented lines in a random pattern around the outside edge. Bake the clay.
3. Cut the stickers into small geometric shapes and attach to the frame after it has cooled.

Mary and Ivy love the campus and their new apartment.
It's the studying that they are not so crazy about.

MATERIALS

- 12" x 12" (30.5 x 30.5 cm) taupe paper for the background
- solid papers: green and melon
- print papers: pink and lavender
- black chipboard
- embossing grains: green, lavender, cream, and blue
- alphabet rub-ons
- alphabet rubber stamps
- computer printer

HIGHER EDUCATION

Scatter these stained-glass leaves about the page and earn credit toward your collage degree.

MELTED EMBOSSING GRAINS look remarkably similar to opaque glass. Use them liberally for this technique. The templates for the leaf overlays can be found on page 199. From the black chipboard, cut one Leaf 1. Cut out the inside shapes to make the veins. From the pink print paper, cut one Leaf 1. Align the edges, and tape the print leaf to the back of the hollow leaf. Repeat to make a second leaf. From the black chipboard, use Leaf 2 to cut a shaped window. (Refer to page 119 for Stained Glass.) Place the leaf on a square of green paper and draw the leaf outline. Sprinkle green and lavender embossing grains over the marked area and apply heat to melt them. Attach the window on the enamel shape

and trim the edges to match. From the black chipboard, cut one Leaf 3. Cut out the inside shapes to make the veins. Place the leaf on a rectangle of green paper and draw the leaf outline. Sprinkle the cream embossing grains on the leaf sections, and sprinkle the blue embossing grains on the background sections. Apply heat to melt the grains and attach the chipboard leaf on the enamel leaf. Tear a border around the leaf. Tear long and short strips from the green and melon papers and apply embossing grains to some. Noting overlaps, arrange and attach the strips, leaves, and photos to the page. Use rubber stamps and rub-on letters to make the title on the lavender paper. Trim around it and attach it to the page.

ter lunch we went downtown and brought a new meaning to "Shop 'til you Drop".

MATERIALS

- 12" x 12" (30.5 x 30.5 cm) papers: taupe and plum for the background
- solid papers: pink, gray, blue, orange, and white
- print papers: gold and taupe
- gold fine glitter
- preprinted caption box
- computer printer

SHOPPING NIRVANA

Throw everything you know about glitter out the window. Then use fine gold grains to highlight this space-age page.

FLUID GEOMETRIC SHAPES were a '70s design staple. Make companion pages with stylized triangles or rectangles. Cut irregular disk shapes from the plum paper. Place the plum paper on the taupe paper. Layer scraps of colored papers between the shaped windows and the background paper. Attach the colored scraps and the plum paper to the background paper. Cut smaller disks from the papers and attach them in selected recessed areas. Cut rings and small disks from a double-sided adhesive sheet. Remove the backing paper and press the shapes in place in selected areas. (Refer to page 120 for Glitter Art.) Remove the protective paper and sprinkle glitter on the exposed adhesive. Remove the excess glitter. Print the title on the white paper and trim around it. Attach the photos, title, and caption box to the page.

IT ALMOST FEELS LIKE FLYING!

MATERIALS

- 12" x 12" (30.5 x 30.5 cm) papers: multi circles and pink print for the background
- white paper
- craft foam: light green, medium green, and blue
- green acrylic paint
- paper tag
- foam adhesive spacers
- computer printer

MOVING PICTURES

Get carried away with paint that almost has a mind of its own.

THE ONLY SKILL REQUIRED for this painting technique is a steady hand. Cut the sides from the pink print paper and attach it to the circles paper. Cut wavy strips from the light green and medium green craft foam. Drop paint beads on the background page and attach the strips on and near the beads. (Refer to page 117 for Paint Art.) Drop additional beads on the strips. Let dry. Cut a curved corner shape from the blue craft foam and attach it to the corner. Print the title on the white paper and trim around it. Attach the photos, paper tag, and title to the page. The photos overlap the foam and require adhesive spacers under the unsupported corners.

MATERIALS

- 12" x 12" (30.5 x 30.5 cm) papers: turquoise print and denim for the background
- print papers: purple and pink
- denim swatch
- tan print fabric
- acrylic paint: lavender, blue, gold, and black
- key charms
- novelty papers: shoes and stockings, color block, and text
- alphabet stickers
- wood dowel
- fine-gauge gold wire
- black colored pencil
- pink paper tag

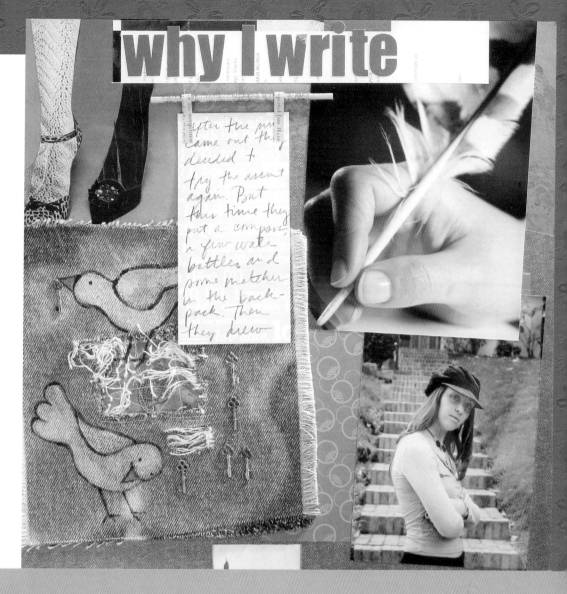

WHY I WRITE

Old jeans never die—they just fade away. (And then come back as album art.)

THE BEST WAY TO AGE DENIM is through years of wear and tear. If you can't wait that long, use the bleaching technique. Also try sanding the raised seams with sandpaper. Trim a curved edge in the top of the denim paper and attach it to the turquoise paper. Trim the denim fabric to the desired size and treat it with bleach if desired. (Refer to page 116 for Distressed Denim.) Cut a window in the center and fray the outside edges and cut edges of the window. Place the tan print fabric behind the window and machine stitch through both layers. The templates for the birds are found on page 201.

Paint the birds on the denim and let dry. Stitch the keys onto the denim. Trim the purple print and the shoes and stockings to the desired sizes. Noting the overlaps, arrange and attach the trimmed papers, denim, the tag, and photos to the page. Trim the edges flush with the page. Wrap the wire around the dowel. Make tabs with strips of text print paper and hang a pink print rectangle from the dowel. Attach the dowel to the page and write the message on the rectangle. Cut a strip for the title from the color block paper and attach it to the page. Press the stickers in place for the title.

EAT YOUR VEGGIES

Give peas a chance…and broccoli, carrots, and peppers.

THE PRINTED PEPPERS are the tip-off to a '70s-style page, along with the color block background and bubble letters. Cut a wide strip from the lavender paper and attach it to the top of the green paper. Cut a rectangle from the pink paper and trim one corner. Cut a curved corner shape from the pink paper. Cut a curved border shape from the blue paper. Cut the peppers in half and dip them in the acrylic paint. (Refer to page 118 for Vegetable Prints.) Press dipped edges on the shapes to make prints. Let dry. Also print the green pepper on the gold and blue papers. Let dry and trim the edges and centers from the printed shapes. The templates for the vegetables are found on page 201. Paint the carrots, peas, and broccoli on the white paper. Let dry and trim around the edges to make silhouette shapes. Cut a curved shape from the flower print paper and cut a length of ricrac. Noting overlaps, arrange and attach the printed shapes, painted shapes, curved shape, photos, and ricrac to the page. Attach the die-cut letters to the page and press the alphabet stickers in place. Use the pencil to write the caption.

MATERIALS

- 12" x 12" (30.5 x 30.5 cm) papers: green and lavender for the background

- solid papers: pink, light blue, gold, and white

- flower print paper

- peppers: green and jalapeño

- acrylic paint: lavender, gold, orange, light green, dark green, and white

- blue ricrac

- sticker alphabet

- die cuts: alphabet, broccoli, and carrot

- black colored pencil

MATERIALS

- 12" x 12" (30.5 x 30.5 cm) wave print and green stripe papers for the background
- solid papers: gold, purple, black, and mint
- print accent paper
- circle and square die cuts
- green velvet (part rayon or silk)
- vine foam stamp
- alphabet stencil
- black marker
- white marker
- embellishments
- old CD
- black printing ink
- text paper

LONG LIVE ROCK

The hits just keep on coming with a page dedicated to the musician in us all.

KEEP TRUE TO THE TIMES and make an LP from a CD. Just blacken an old CD with ink and make a label from a magazine scrap. To make the page, cut sections from the green stripe, gold, and accent papers. Cut a rectangle from the black paper and attach it and the trimmed sections to the page. Place the foam stamp face up on the ironing board. (Refer to page 121 for Embossed Velvet.) Place the velvet wrong side up on the stamp and press. Move the stamp around the velvet and repeat to create the desired pattern. Cut around the stamped pattern. Coat the back of the velvet with spray adhesive and press it in place on the page. Cut circles from the purple and gold papers and place them behind the die-cut circles. Attach the CD, circles, and photos to the page. Trim the overlapping edges. Trim the CD with a metal-edge ruler and craft knife. It will require several passes with the knife to cut through the plastic. Cut a circle from the text paper and punch a hole in the center. Attach it to the CD. Use the white marker to write the first two words of the title and stencil the last word. With a craft knife, cut through all layers of a selected letter and back the area with mint paper.

What comes after the corn dog, the cotton candy, and the Pepto?

MATERIALS

- 12" x 12" (30.5 x 30.5 cm) white paper for the background
- solid papers: pink and white
- dot paper
- stamped medallion
- gold tissue
- fabrics: pink, paisley, and denim
- colored pencils: pink, brown, and green
- lavender craft foam
- flower sticker
- computer printer

CARNIVAL

Take a walk on the wild side of the boardwalk, the side covered with denim and paisley.

WHEN ATTACHING THE PAISLEY shapes to the denim, stitch through the foam edges or use strips of double-sided adhesive. To make the page, cut large sections from the pink fabric and gold tissue. Cut a small section from the paisley fabric. Cut a short strip from the dot paper. Noting overlaps, arrange and attach the fabrics, tissue, dot paper, and photos to the page. Treat the denim with bleach if desired. (Refer to page 116 for Distressed Denim.) Cut irregular shapes from the denim. Cut slits in selected areas and fray the cut edges and slits. Color the medallion and attach it to the pink paper.

Trim the paper, leaving a border, and machine stitch the border to a denim shape. Cut sections from the paisley fabric and coat the backs with spray adhesive. Press them onto the craft foam. Trim around the shapes, leaving a narrow border of foam. Attach the shapes to the denim sections. Coat the backs of the sections with spray adhesive and press them in place on the bottom of the page. Print the title and captions on the white paper, trim around them, and attach them to the page. Press the sticker in place by the title.

MATERIALS

- 12" x 12" (30.5 x 30.5 cm) lavender paper for the background
- solid papers: white, green, and turquoise
- assorted paper accent scraps of coordinating prints and colors
- mulberry tissue papers: white, pink, and lavender
- dimensional paint: periwinkle, purple, peach, and green
- acrylic paint: periwinkle, blue, lavender, and yellow
- party invitation
- chipboard

PARTY PAINT

Decorate your party with bold color and painted frills.

SINCE THIS BACKGROUND is a riot of color, few elements are needed to complete the page. Tear sections from the turquoise and green papers. Cut sections from the accent papers. Noting overlaps, arrange and attach them to the page. Place strips of white mulberry tissue on the work surface and drop acrylic paint beads along the top edges. (Refer to page 117 for Paint Art.) Using a strip of chipboard as a squeegee, pull the paint down the page. Let dry. Cut circles from the pink and lavender mulberry tissue. With the dimensional paint, draw flowers and/or medallion designs in the centers of the circles. Let dry. Trim the white paper to the desired size. Arrange and attach the tissue strips, tissue circles, white paper, photos, and invitation to the page.

The perfect **sunset**

MATERIALS

- 12" x 12" (30.5 x 30.5 cm) light blue paper for the background
- 12" x 12" (30.5 x 30.5 cm) section from a fuzzy poster
- colored markers or printing inks: light blue and dark blue
- beaded fringe
- pink quilling strip
- purple paper
- preprinted title
- cardboard or foam adhesive spacers

FUZZY SUNSET

Your true love's eyes are deep pools of blue. And coincidentally, so is the ink that colors this retro poster.

THE BLACK DYE in the velvet finish of the poster will rub off on your hands, so wash them often when assembling this page. Cut a window in the poster for the photo. Color the poster with the markers or ink pads. (Refer to page 121 for Embossed Velvet.) Attach the poster to the light blue paper. Cut a length of fringe that is slightly longer than the photo, and attach the fringe and the photo to the page. Since the photo overlaps the fringe, the photo needs to be mounted with spacers, such as cardboard or foam adhesive spacers. Cut the purple paper to the desired size and attach it, the title, and the pink strip to the page.

MATERIALS

- 12" x 12" (30.5 x 30.5 cm) tan print paper for the background

- solid papers: tan, brown, white, green, lavender, orange, and peach

- silver brushed paper

- flocked polka dot paper

- cream mulberry tissue

- orange stitched ribbon

- preprinted message tags

- embroidery floss: dark brown and light brown

- computer printer

books AND friends

HANGING OUT IN A MUSTY
BOOK STORE
WAITING FOR THE MAN OF
MY DREAMS, (RHETT BUTLER) TO
WALK INTO MY LIFE.

BOOK TALK

She must have a way with words, and you must have a way with color and design.

THIS DESIGN IS MADE with colored paper representing the glass. (Refer to page 119 for Stained Glass.) Choose colors that will contrast with the overlay paper. Cut three squares from the brown paper. The template for the window overlay is found on page 202. Cut out the inside shapes to create the overlays. Place one overlay on the white paper and trace the shapes on the paper. Used the traced shapes as templates for the color areas. Cut the shapes from the selected colors and attach them to a second piece of white paper. Attach the overlay to the colored paper. Trim the edges to match. Tear a section from the mulberry tissue and cut irregular shapes from the flocked polka dot and tan papers. Noting overlaps, arrange and attach the tissue, paper shapes, and photo to the page. Arrange the colored window and overlays on the page with the edges overlapping. Trim the edges and add them to the composition. Attach them to the page. Cut a short length of ribbon and hand stitch it to the page with the dark brown floss. Pierce four holes at the top and bottom edges of the photo. With the threads crossing at the center, stitch the thread through the pierced holes. Tape the ends to the back of the page to secure them. Cut a short strand of light brown floss and use it to tie a knot around the threads. Print the caption on the peach paper and trim around it. Attach the title tags and caption to the page.

ROAD TRIP

Hit the road, Jack, and then come back and chronicle the fun.

MATERIALS

- 12" x 12" (30.5 x 30.5 cm) papers: gold print and peach for the background
- solid papers: gold, green, black, white, and blue
- magenta print paper
- preprinted title strip
- blue glitter
- blue craft foam
- embellishments: kites and butterfly
- black fine-point marker
- computer printer

A CURVED PAPER HIGHWAY makes us wonder what is waiting around the next bend. To make the page, cut the right edge from the peach paper and attach it to the gold print paper. Cut squares from the gold and green papers. Draw ray shapes on the green square and cut them from the paper with a craft knife. Place the green paper on the gold paper and skew the edges. Draw the rays on the gold paper and cover them with double-sided adhesive. (Refer to page 120 for Glitter Art.) Remove the protective paper to expose the adhesive and align the rays. Sprinkle glitter on the exposed adhesive and remove the excess. Realign the squares and attach them, the title strip, and the photo to the page. The templates for the car and the road are found on page 203. Cut the car from the foam and the remaining shapes from the designated colors of paper. Print the captions on the white paper and trim around them. Cut strips from the black and blue papers. Noting overlaps, arrange and attach the car, road, paper strips, and caption strips to the page. Secure the kites and butterfly to the page with strips of double-sided adhesive. Use the marker to write the text.

MATERIALS

- 12" x 12" (30.5 x 30.5 cm) light pink paper for the background
- red cabbage
- pink paper
- assorted scraps of colored and novelty papers
- text paper
- flower die cut
- paper mat
- rayon ribbons: lavender, tan, and striped
- green grosgrain ribbon
- purple sequins
- gray acrylic paint
- computer printer

SPRING CELEBRATION OF LOVE

Style and produce collide to make a stunning wallpaper print background.

PLAY WITH YOUR FOOD and you may be delighted with the results. Cut the cabbage into sections with flat sides. (Refer to page 118 for Vegetable Prints.) Press the flat sides in a random pattern on the pink paper and let dry. Cut strips from the paper scraps. Cut lengths from the rayon ribbons and secure them to the paper strips with loose knots. Cut a length of green ribbon and hand stitch sequins to the ribbon.

Tear the text paper into sections and cut the paper scraps into the desired shapes. Print the caption on the pink paper and trim around it. Noting overlaps, arrange and attach the paper mat, photo, caption, and paper scraps to the page. Trim the overlapping edges. Also attach the ribbons and flower die cut to the page. Paint the title.

CONTEMPORARY STYLE

THE FUN OF PAPER scrapping is that it is always changing. As a cultural movement, it has drawn in many enthusiasts and taken us on a swift ride of evolving tastes and techniques. To describe today's style, it is important to take into account where we started and to ask where we are going. As a graphic artist, I design a scrapbook page as if it were a page in a magazine, taking into account the photo, title, text, and illustration. When I consider that it should look good and convey a message in the same way that a magazine page looks good and sells an idea or product, the concept and the execution become clear. Throw in all the treatment techniques and the three-dimensional accents

and it becomes more complicated and more fun. For example, a miniature satin wedding dress sold as a page accent, realistic right down to the lace collar and pearl buttons, makes me appreciate the sophistication of the current marketplace, and the potential for bigger and better things to come. My basic magazine page has now turned into a complex layered collage of manipulated paper treatments topped off with dazzling appliqués.

Thus the techniques presented in this chapter are divided into two categories: paper treatments and page add-ons. And two styles, spare and cluttered, are shown in the layout pages.

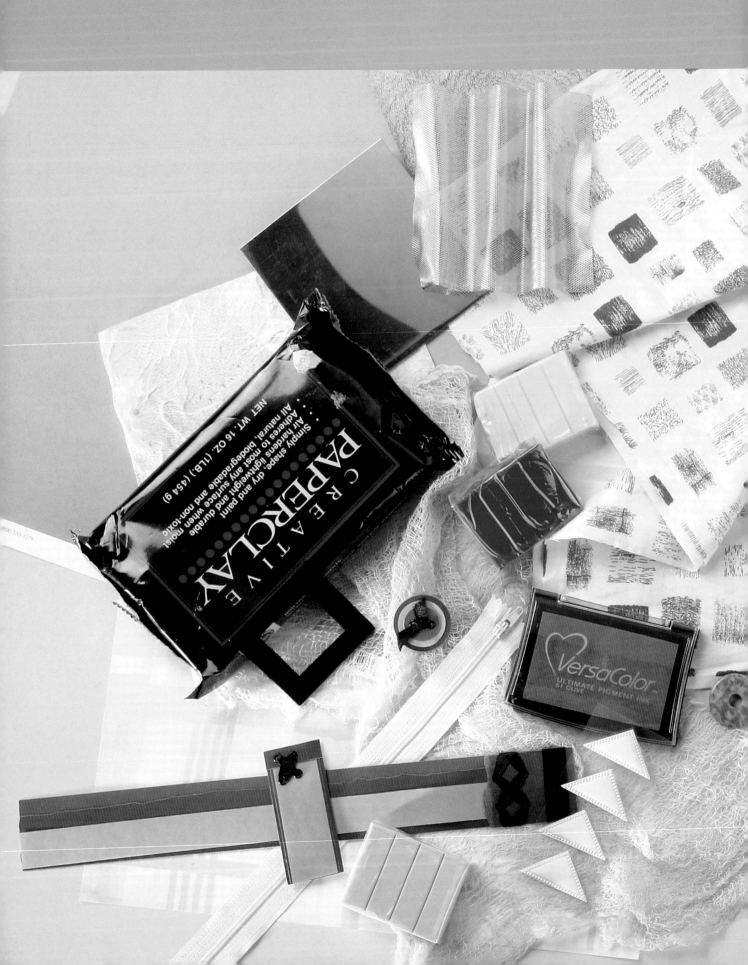

Today's pages often fall into the "less is more" category of flat backgrounds and spare accents. For this style, use simple geometric shapes and accent with glass or plastic details. The opposite approach is also popular: covering every last corner of the page with 3-D treatments and paper graffiti. Add soft, wispy texture with hand-dyed gauze or add hard-edge drama with industrial wire and folded metal screen. Some surefire ways to select colors are by going monochromatic, using complementary colors, or combining different hues of the same value.

technique:
PAPER PIECING

Paper piecing consists of cutting individual shapes from colored papers and assembling them to complete a design. Flat areas of color mean that a finished paper-pieced image resembles a stencil, silk screen, or fabric appliqué. In fact, the name was borrowed from fabric piecing done by quilters. Some shapes will overlap others, so allow excess paper along the edges that will be covered by adjoining shapes. Use contrasting colors of paper to add definition and depth to the design.

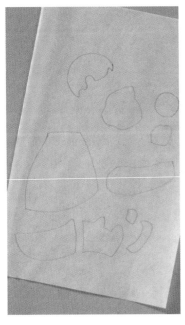

STEP 1

Noting that some shapes may overlap others, draw the shapes on tracing paper.

STEP 2

Cut out the shapes from the tracing paper, then match them to the selected papers.

STEP 3

Cut shapes from the colored papers.

STEP 4

Assemble the shapes to complete the design.

See the projects on pages 30, 85, 153, 155, 161, 170, and 172 that feature Paper Piecing.

technique:
WEAVING

Weaving has long served as a metaphor for melding memories or entwining souls. When worked with paper, it is a way to create intriguing patterns. To add interest, start with a straightforward over/under sequence, and then skew the grid by weaving the strips at an angle. Experiment with bold print patterns and a variety of paper weights. For example, weaving tissue strips between paper slits results in a much tighter weave.

STEP 1

Cut narrow strips from selected papers.

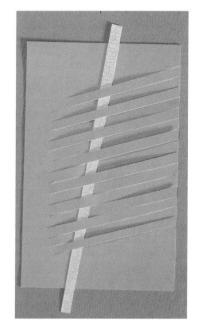

STEP 2

Cut slits in the background paper and weave a strip with a simple over/under pattern between the slits.

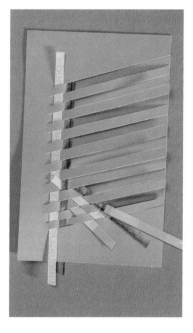

STEP 3

Change the direction of the weave if desired with shorter paper strips.

STEP 4

Finish the weaving and attach a large section of double-sided adhesive to the back of the weaving to hold the strips and slit edges in place. Add any desired accents.

See the projects on pages 153, 164, and 169 that feature Weaving.

technique:
DIP-DYED PAPER

There are many ways to color paper, including painting, inking, and coloring with pencils or markers. But the easiest and most effective method is to dip it in a shallow dish filled with dye. A straightforward process with no skill required, dip-dyeing can be used to create a variety of showstopping effects.

STEP 1

Mix the dye to the desired strength and dip the paper in the dye. Remove the paper from the dye and place it on paper towels to dry.

SAMPLES 1 and 2

For a soft edge, wet the paper before dipping. For a crisp edge, dip dry paper.

SAMPLE 3

For a veined pattern, crinkle the paper into a small ball and dip the ball in the dye. It may be necessary to open the ball and dip it several times to cover the entire surface of the paper.

STEP 2

Use the paper for folded or paper-pieced projects.

See the projects on pages 34, 41, 159, and 166 that feature Dip-Dyed Paper.

technique:
FAUX HANDMADE PAPER

Making handmade paper sounds like one of those crafts that you just have to try—that is, until you actually try it. Making pulp is messy and time-consuming, mixing the pulp with water and binder is messy and time-consuming, and compressing wet pulp between drying screens is messy and time-consuming. And waiting for the paper to dry? Forget about it. By the time it is actually dry, you have forgotten that you made it in the first place. An easy way to achieve the same look is with that most common of household commodities, toilet tissue. Douse it with liquid starch for textured paper or add diluted white glue for textured paper strewn with stray bits of thread or confetti.

STEP 1
Mix one part white craft glue and three parts water.

STEP 2
Arrange a length of toilet tissue on a plastic sheet.

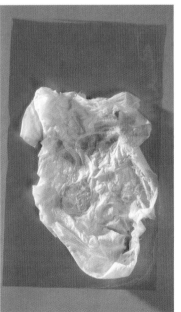

STEP 3
Drip the diluted glue on the paper and shape as desired. After shaping, add paper confetti, threads, etc. Let dry.

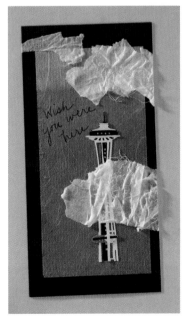

STEP 4
Cut or tear the edges of the paper to the desired shapes and attach them to the page.

See the projects on pages 34, 174, and 179 that feature Faux Handmade Paper.

technique:
CLAY ART

Turn crop time into playtime by working with these malleable and inviting media. Two types are featured—polymer clay and air-drying modeling clay—and both can be rolled thin enough to make decorations for a flat page. Polymer clay has an even texture and comes in a rainbow of colors. It can be twisted, folded, etched, and carved, and it stays soft until baked. Air-drying modeling clay has a grainy texture and is a neutral color of ivory. It is slightly less elastic than polymer clay but can be shaped, etched, and sanded, and it is extremely lightweight when dry.

SAMPLE 1

To make marbled shapes from polymer clay, knead the clay and roll it into tubes. Twist and fold the tubes together to achieve the desired pattern. Cut slices from the clay, place the slices next to each other on the work surface, and roll them to join. Cut the silhouette shapes from the clay and bake.

SAMPLE 2

Other techniques for polymer clay include embedding accents in the clay before baking, and creating a ragged edge. To achieve this look, tear a thin sheet of clay and place a section of it on a contrasting color. Roll both to meld the clay sections together. Trim the edges and bake.

SAMPLE 3

To make silhouette shapes from air-drying clay, roll out the clay and cut the shape. After the clay has dried, sand the edges or trim them with a craft knife.

SAMPLE 4

To make etched drawings on air-drying clay, roll out the clay and draw a design on the surface of the clay with a stylus. Paint the dried clay with watercolor paints or gouache.

See the projects on pages 33, 98, 152, 155, and 177 that feature Clay Art.

technique:
STITCHED PAPER

Hang on tightly and push your pages through a sewing machine for crazy stitched seam accents. When machine stitching paper to join layers or to add embellishments, keep three things in mind: the stitches should be far enough apart to prevent tearing, the thread ends should be secured to the back of the page after stitching, and the paper will dull your sewing machine needle. Hand stitching is also a great way to enhance paper and is done with a simple over/under running stitch. Pierce holes in the right side of the project before stitching and use them as insertion points when bringing the needle from the back to the front and from the front to the back. A third stitching option is to punch holes or insert eyelets in the paper and then stitch through the holes with ribbon or floss.

STEP 1

Assemble papers and ribbon of different textures and opacity.

TECHNIQUE 1

Cut or tear the materials and layer them. Machine stitch the papers and ribbon in place.

TECHNIQUE 2

Cut or tear the materials and layer them. Use a running stitch to hand stitch the papers and ribbon in place.

COMBINED TECHNIQUES

Combine hand stitching, machine stitching, and stitched eyelets in a quirky composition.

See the projects on pages 61, 153, 159, 167, and 173 that feature Stitched Paper.

technique:
FILM OVERLAY

This clever technique allows for replicating the articulated details of leaves and flowers with the help of acrylic paint and plastic film. The film is packaged in rolls and is sold in paper and craft stores for the purpose of preserving paper documents. It has the right amount of grip to pull paint from the plants, and a transparent finish to show off the results. Choose flowers and leaves that are dry and that have a smooth finish. Leaves with a fuzzy surface won't release the paint. Use only undiluted acrylic paint, which has just the right opacity and elasticity. By following these steps you can make a beautiful and detailed bouquet without adding bulk to the page.

STEP 1
Choose the flowers and leaves.

STEP 2
Pull the leaves and blossoms from the stems and paint them with acrylic paint. Let dry.

STEP 3
Coat the backs of the leaves and blossoms with spray adhesive and press them in place. Remove the backing from the film and place the film on the leaves and flowers. Using your finger as a brayer, rub the film that is directly over the painted surfaces. Slowly peel the film from the leaves and flowers to lift the paint from them.

STEP 4
Press the film on the selected paper. To accent the edge of the film, color over it and the background paper with a soft colored pencil. This creates a two-toned border because the color will be lighter on the film and darker on the paper.

See the projects on pages 158 and 178 that feature Film Overlay.

technique:
METAL ART

Looking for something flashy or sleek to add to your pages? Discover gold (copper, silver, and aluminum) in lightweight metal sheeting. It comes in a variety of colors and finishes, and it can be cut with ordinary utility scissors. Or add accents made from shaped sheet metal, shiny metal mesh, or embossed tin tiles.

STEP 1

Assemble the metal sheeting, mesh, and/or accents.

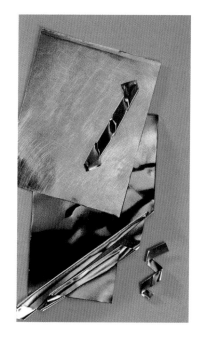

TECHNIQUES 1 AND 2

Scuff the metal surface with fine sandpaper or fold the sheeting.

TECHNIQUE 3

Emboss the metal by lightly hammering fork tines or a hole punch tool onto the surface.

SAMPLES

Layer contrasting colors or add metal accents.

See the projects on pages 155, 156, 157, 165, and 175 that feature Metal Art.

technique:
RECYCLED ART

Have you ever wished that you could think outside the box? Well, think like someone who was never in the box (or any other confining shape with hard edges and right angles.) You can do this by looking at everyday objects for decoration rather than for utility. Choose objects or materials with a low profile that will fit on the page. Some nonporous surfaces, such as plastic or metal, should be attached to the page with double-sided adhesive strips.

STEP 1

Choose the materials. Look around your house and force yourself to notice things that have become too familiar to you.

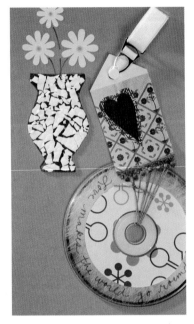

SAMPLES

Wash and dry eggshells and use them as mosaic tiles, suspend a paper tag from a garter, or sand an old CD and write a message around the outside edge.

SAMPLES

Trim rug gripper rubber and fill the holes with dimensional paint. Attach small objects to the page with the plastic mesh of a hair roller. Decorate a matchbook and cut a food wrapper into a decorative shape.

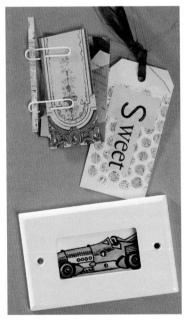

SAMPLES

Use paper clips to hold stacks of decorative papers. Apply ink to the bumpy side of bubble paper and use it to stamp patterns on tags or background paper. Make a sleek frame from a light switch cover.

See the projects on pages 154, 156, 157, 159, 163, and 168 that feature Recycled Art.

technique:
HARDWARE
ACCENTS

Solid metal fasteners become more interesting when juxtaposed against fragile paper. Use them in unexpected ways and secure them to the page with wire, ribbon, brads, or paper strips.

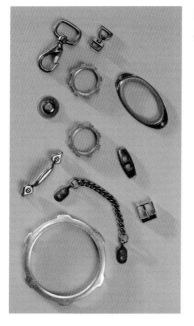

STEP 1

Choose the hardware.

SAMPLES

Attach a label holder with fine wire and a hook with an adhesive-backed paper strip. Secure a mini handle to the page with bendable prongs.

SAMPLES

Highlight a stamped image and candle stickers with threaded washers. Secure a chain and label with brads.

SAMPLES

Hold buckles and slides in place with strips of fabric and leather.

See the projects on pages 171 and 176 that feature Hardware Accents.

THE KEY TO MY HEART

A cryptic message for your one and only. (Refer to page 146 for Clay Art.)

1. Knead the clay and roll it to approximately ¼" (6 mm) thick. Cut the shapes from the clay.
2. Apply dark ink to a face rubber stamp and press the face into the soft clay. Press the flat side of a metal hook into the soft clay. Bake the clay and let it cool.
3. Glue the hook to the plaque. Attach the stickers and key.

TORN EDGE CLAY FRAME

This easy technique can be used to make a one-of-a-kind graphic statement. (Refer to page 146 for Clay Art.)

1. Knead the blue clay and roll it to approximately ⅛" (1 cm) thick. Repeat with the green clay. Carefully stretch the green clay until it tears.
2. Place the green layer on the blue layer with the blue clay exposed behind the torn edge. Roll lightly to meld the colors.
3. Cut a square with a centered window from the clay. Crimp the outside edges with a flat tool, bake, and let cool. For a brushed surface, sand the frame with fine sandpaper. Tape the photo to the back of the frame.

PIECED AND PINNED CARD

This simple card serves as a mini bulletin board for a mini photo and pins.

1. Layer a patterned fabric rectangle and a solid one on the paper and stitch a grid pattern through all layers.
2. Cut through the top layer only of selected squares and remove the fabric to reveal the patterned fabric.
3. With small safety pins, pin small snippets of coordinating fabric to a vertical row of stitched squares. Stitch a narrow border along the opposite side. Pull the thread ends to the back of the card and tape them to secure. Trim the thread ends and pin the photo to the fabric.

COTTON SWAB FABRIC CARD

Cotton swabs share center stage on this sunny card.

1. Cut and arrange fabric strips and rectangles on the paper. Cut a round flower shape from a selected color and trim the photo to fit within the circle.

2. Using a straight stitch and a zigzag stitch, stitch through all layers to secure. (Refer to page 147 for Stitched Paper.) Cut a 4" (10.2 cm) strip and a 2½" (6.4 cm) square from coordinating fabrics. Place the strip vertically on the bottom of the card. Center and place the square diagonally on the strip, and stitch from the left corner to the right corner. Fold the corners over the cotton swabs and knot the strip ends. Pull the thread ends to the back of the card and tape them to secure. Trim the thread ends.

COLOR BLOCK WEAVE

Paper and fabric shall meet when blended together as a winning mini weave.

1. Cut a wide strip of patterned fabric. Cut slits at each end, leaving 1½" (3.8 cm) in the center of the strip that is uncut. Cut narrow strips from the patterned paper. Secure the uncut center of the strip to the card with double-sided adhesive.

2. Weave the paper strips through one cut end of the fabric strips. Wrap the ends of the paper strips and the top of the fabric strip to the back of the card and secure with tape. Attach the photo to the card.

VERY MERRY MAT

Many treatments celebrate a single event—the annual arrival of Santa Claus! (Refer to page 142 for Paper Piecing and to page 147 for Stitched Paper.)

1. Cut paper triangles and narrow paper strips. Arrange and attach them to the mat. Punch holes in the mat and sprinkle the edge with stamped snowflakes.

2. With a large needle, punch three vertical rows of holes in a strip of contrasting paper. With yarn, stitch two sets of four horizontal stitches, and tie the stitches together with short lengths of contrasting yarn. Attach the stitched strip to the bottom of the mat.

Mini Projects

Dinner Is Served

Have an appetite for miniatures?

1. Draw a plate and utensils on the etched side of shrink plastic. Note that the plastic will shrink to fifty percent of the original size.
2. Cut around the outside edges and bake the shapes according to the manufacturer's directions.
3. Make a folded napkin and menu from white vellum. Arrange and attach the plastic shapes, mini candy, napkin, and menu to a decorative tag.

Corrugated Frame

Embossing powder adds a shiny dressed-up finish to humble corrugated paper.

1. Sprinkle pastel embossing powder into the recesses of a corrugated paper mat.
2. Following the manufacturer's directions, heat the powder to dissolve. Let cool, cut out a window, and add embellishments.

Do Judge a Book by Its Cover

A favorite cloth book cover is easy to cut and paste, the old-fashioned way. (Refer to page 150 for Recycled Art.)

1. Using a craft knife, cut a rectangle from an old cloth-bound book cover. Cut through the cloth layer only, and remove it from the chipboard backing.
2. Cut a large and a small shaped window from the cloth. Place a length of metallic ribbon behind the small window.
3. Arrange and secure the cut cloth, die cut, and photo to the page. Slide the pencils under the ribbon and secure them to the page with narrow strips of double-sided adhesive.

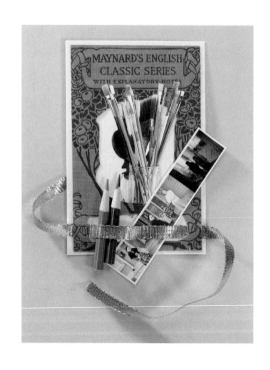

Wrapped Tile Tag

Every artist knows that haphazard arrangements are often the most carefully planned. (Refer to page 146 for Clay Art.)

1. Knead the clay and roll it to approximately ¼" (6 mm) thick. Cut small tiles from the clay and repeat with assorted colors. Bake the clay and let it cool.
2. Attach the tiles to a paper rectangle with small squares of double-sided adhesive.
3. Layer a scrap of tissue and the tiled paper on a rectangle of corrugated paper and wrap all layers with hemp twine. Glue the photo to the tag.

Affirmation Tag

Keep it simple, sweetie. (Refer to page 149 for Metal Art.)

1. Attach the caption to a metal rectangle with glue dots.
2. Cut patterned paper strips and a red paper heart. Arrange and attach the strips and heart to the tag.
3. With small squares of double-sided adhesive, attach metal rectangle, metal corner, and glass blocks to the tag.

Big-Top Birthday Cake

Make a birthday card with animal attraction. (Refer to page 142 for Paper Piecing.)

1. Cut the pieces for the cake and plate.
2. Noting the overlaps, layer and secure the pieces to each other. Attach a novelty paper tiger to the card and trim the edges.
3. Attach the cake to the card and press the stickers in place for the caption.

MINI PROJECTS

EAST MEETS WEST METAL COLLAGE

Embrace the zen of mixed-media scrapping. (Refer to page 149 for Metal Art.)

1. Attach a small piece of aluminum mesh to the corner of the page with a square of double-sided adhesive.
2. Press a scrap of tissue on the adhesive that is exposed behind the mesh.
3. Arrange and attach the paper scraps, circle die cut, metal triptych frame, and hinge on the paper. Use a marker to write the message.

BEST OF THE MESH

Spin this old CD into a hip recycled frame. (Refer to page 149 for Metal Art.) (Refer to page 150 for Recycled Art.)

1. Cut a 1¼" x 16" (3.1 x 40.6 cm) strip of aluminum mesh.
2. Crimp the strip evenly around the edge of a CD. Slide the corners of the photo under the mesh to secure.

LASHED LEATHER FRAMES

Fabric and leather combine in an easy mix of colors and textures.

1. Cut a fabric shape that matches the leather frame. Cut a narrow strip of leather.
2. Loop the fabric around one corner and wrap it with the leather strip to secure. Knot and trim the ends. Tape paper backing to the back and add objects or artwork.

ALTERED BOOK FRAME

Cross over into the world of altered books with this simple project. (Refer to page 144 for Dip-Dyed Paper.) (Refer to page 150 for Recycled Art.)

1. Roll a section of gauze and dip it into a shallow bowl of dye. After the gauze is saturated, blot between paper towels and let dry.
2. Using a craft knife, cut a rectangle from an old cloth-bound book cover. Cut through the cloth layer only and remove it to expose the chipboard backing.
3. Weave twigs through the gauze and the outer edges. Coat the back of the gauze with spray adhesive and wrap the gauze edges around the sides of the book. Trim the top and bottom edges and attach the photo and paper slide to the cover.

SPACE-AGE METAL TAG

Modern scrapping meets George Jetson. (Refer to page 149 for Metal Art.) (Refer to page 151 for Hardware Accents.)

1. Make a stylized mini mat from sandpaper.
2. Rub decorator chalk on the mat on selected areas, and wrap the mat with fine gold wire.
3. Tape the photo and metal strips to the back of the mat. Attach the caption.

MINIMALIST METAL FRAME

A simple frame proves that form follows function. (Refer to page 149 for Metal Art.)

1. Attach the photo to a metal rectangle with a square of double-sided adhesive. Attach a paper strip to the bottom of the photo.
2. Bend a solid and a mesh metal strip and slide them on the sides of the metal. Secure the strips to the back of the metal with double-sided adhesive.

BASKET TAG

Climb higher by making stacked paper tags.

1. Fold a two-toned paper square in half and in half again. Rotate the square, tuck the side corners in, and fold the top corner down to make a triangle.
2. Cut a handle and base to make a basket. Attach the basket shapes and mini tags to the large tag. Add a sticker, stamped name, and wire hanger.

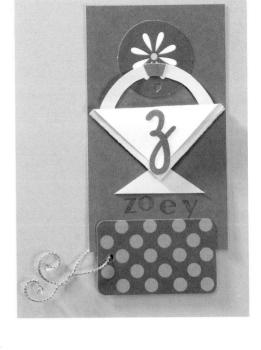

TRIFOLD DOG TAG

Make an I-love-you tag for your best friend.

1. Cut a window in a trifold tag. Center and attach the photo to the center section.
2. Add embellishments, including a folded ruffle, metal washer, and captions.
3. Hang the tag from a length of knotted and pinned metallic ricrac.

CASCADE TAG

A little plastic film and a little colored pencil make this snowman shine. (Refer to page 148 for Film Overlay.)

1. Cut a smaller snowman silhouette from clear adhesive film. Center and press in place on the snowman tag.
2. With a soft colored pencil, color along the edges. Add paper twigs for arms and a paper hat. Thread the tag on a strip of quilling paper along with assorted small tags.

Museum Quality Notebook

What better place to jot down personal notes than in a personalized notebook?

1. Cut matching paper rectangles. Punch holes along the top edges.
2. Wrap a length of copper wire around a pencil. Align the holes in the rectangles and twist the coiled wire to thread it through the holes.
3. Attach the photo and the decorative papers to the front cover. Tie a short pencil to the coiled wire with a length of ribbon and use a pencil to write the message. To suggest thickness, add foam adhesive spacers between the covers.

Time Flies Tag

An old watchband helps illustrate a universal truth. (Refer to page 144 for Dip-Dyed Paper.) (Refer to page 150 for Recycled Art.)

1. Dip a paper scrap in green dye and let dry.
2. Attach the lengths of the watchband with strips of double-sided adhesive.
3. Make the watch face and wings and secure them over the watchband ends with foam adhesive spacers.

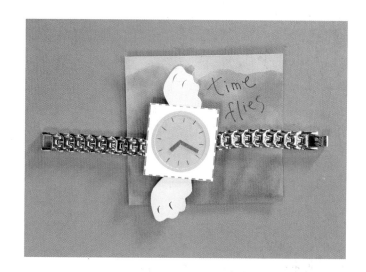

Fire in the Sky

A couching stitch is the secret behind this flashy fireworks mat. (Refer to page 147 for Stitched Paper.)

1. Use a colored pencil to draw a pinwheel shape on the paper. Use a small needle to pierce evenly spaced holes along the marked lines. Place a length of ribbon on the lines and bring the thread from the back to the front of the paper. Wrap the thread around the ribbon and take the thread from the front to the back through the same hole. Repeat stitching through the remaining holes.
2. Backstitch through one row of pierced holes if desired. Add decorative papers and cut a window. Tape the photo to the back of the mat.

PEEKABOO FAT PACKAGE

What is more tantalizing than a wrapped package? You may want to shake this one and then peek through the holes in the paper.

1. Cut a small Fome-cor square and a larger paper square. Center the Fome-cor and mark the paper at the corners.
2. Cut notches to the marks, and score and fold the side flaps. Punch holes in the paper.
3. Wrap the paper around the square and tape the flaps to the back to secure. Tie paper ribbon around the package and add a notched tag.

DOUBLE-DECKER CONE

We all scream for ice cream (and for clever pastel tags). Use this one to satisfy your visual sweet tooth.

1. With a pencil, lightly draw a circle on the tag. Cut a matching circle from a cotton ball. Apply a thin layer of craft glue inside the circle, and press the cotton in place. Let dry.
2. Cut a larger circle from mulberry tissue paper. Coat the back of the paper circle with spray adhesive, center on the cotton, and press the edges to the paper.
3. Repeat with a second circle, and add a paper cone and embellishments. Use a marker to write a caption.

FOLDED FLOWER GARDEN

How does this garden grow? With paper, paint, and a trusty pair of scissors.

1. Cut a 3" (7.6 cm) circle from two-toned paper. Center and draw a 1½" (3.8 cm) circle. Cut evenly spaced notches to the marked line.
2. Paint the right edges of the flaps. Let dry.
3. Working clockwise, fold the flaps to the center of the circle.
4. Fold the edge of the last flap under the edge of the first.
5. Attach the flowers to the page with stems and leaves.

DRAWSTRING CANDY BAG

Present a photo gift that is tucked inside a translucent gift bag.

1. Choose a transparent bag made of organza or cellophane that will showcase the photo and bag inserts. Cut a window in the front of the bag that is slightly smaller than the trimmed photo.
2. Attach narrow strips of double-sided adhesive to the edges of the photo and remove the protective paper layer.
3. Carefully slide the photo in the bag and center it behind the window. Press the edges of the window to the edges of the photo to secure. Insert mini candy in the bag behind the photo.

AVANT ART CARD

Hugs and kisses are represented with letter stickers. Two sets create instant shadows.

1. Attach dot stickers and letters to the paper square. Offset the letter stickers to create shadows.
2. Cut and layer a geometric shape and set of lips. Attach them to the paper and attach the paper to the card. (Refer to page 142 for Paper Piecing.)

LAYOUTS

MATERIALS

- 12" x 12" (30.5 x 30.5 cm) pale pink paper for the background
- white polished paper
- yellow lined paper
- tissue papers: pink, pink print, and yellow
- die-cut eggs
- pink Easter grass
- foam adhesive spacers
- fine white feathers (optional)
- computer printer
- black colored pencil

GOOD EGG HUNTING

Simple, fresh, and inspired. Sprinkle areas of interesting textures around a single strong photo.

To make the layered horizon line, carefully cut around the heads of the photo subjects with a craft knife. Place a rectangle of pink tissue on the top of the photo, lift the cut flap, and slide the tissue edge behind the heads. Cut a notched strip from the print tissue. Cut short, narrow strips from the yellow tissue and place them on the notched strip. (Refer to page 17 for Ruching.) With the sewing machine, run a gathering stitch down the center, and gather to the desired length and fullness. The template for the rabbit is found on page 204. Cut two rabbit shapes from the white paper. Arrange and attach the tissue, photo, and ruched strip to the page. Arrange and attach the grass, eggs, one rabbit, and title to the page. Attach one egg and one rabbit with foam adhesive spacers to add dimension. The feather details are secured to the photo with narrow strips of double-sided adhesive. Print the title, cut it into individual letters, and attach it to the lined paper. Trim the yellow paper and attach it to the page. Use the colored pencil to write the caption. The white feathers are attached to the photo with double-sided adhesive.

MATERIALS

- 12" x 12" (30.5 x 30.5 cm) navy paper for background
- white paper
- blue print vellum
- three-dimensional paper alphabet stickers
- preprinted title strip
- preprinted Mylar caption boxes
- cotton balls
- hairpins
- two aluminum soda cans
- silver eyelets
- candy wrappers
- computer printer

RECYCLED HOUSE

Be it ever so humble, there is no place like a home made from a soda can.

WRAPPERS OR LABELS should reflect your actual tastes. For example, I would rather live in a ketchup house than a mustard one. From the vellum, cut a rectangle with one curved edge and a corner with a curved edge. Cut sections from the candy wrappers. Attach the vellum, candy wrappers, title strip, and photos to the page. The template for the house is found on page 204. Rinse and dry the soda cans. (Refer to page 150 for Recycled Art.) Punch holes in the sides of the cans with an awl and cut two 3" (7.6 cm) squares with metal sheers. Cut the house and roof from the squares. Cut the left and top sides of the door and bend it to the front of the house. Punch holes at the top edge of the house and at the bottom edge of the roof. Align the pieces and join them with the eyelets. Cut flat circles from the cotton balls and secure them to the vellum with the hairpins. Press the alphabet stickers in place on the page. Print the captions on the white paper and trim around them. From the white paper, cut boxes to highlight the clear caption boxes. Arrange and attach the paper boxes, caption boxes, and captions to the page.

LO-51-SS.JPG

ONE IS SILVER AND THE OTHER IS GOLD

Use silver and gold tissue to weave a tribute to a friend.

MATERIALS

- 12" x 12" (30.5 x 30.5 cm) papers: gold and gold print for the background
- gold paper
- tissue paper: silver and gold
- ribbon: cream organza, tan print, gray stripe, and purple stripe
- gray paper mat
- assorted bronze envelopes
- novelty papers: fabric, script, brooch, and watch
- medallion slide jewelry
- computer printer

SAVE YOUR BEST JUNK jewelry and your best paper accents to add to the border. From the right edge of the gold print paper to the center of the page, cut diagonal slits approximately ⅜" (1 cm) wide. (Refer to page 143 for Weaving.) Cut ⅜" (1 cm) strips from the gold and silver tissue. Weave the strips through the slits. Change the direction of the strips if desired. On the back of the page, tape the backs of the strips and tape along the edge of the slits to secure. Attach the woven paper to the gold print paper at an angle and trim the edges to match. Cut the novelty papers and insert them into the envelopes. Attach the mat and photo to the page. Cut lengths of the organza and print ribbons and weave them over and under the envelopes. Cut lengths of the striped ribbons and thread them through the medallion eyelets. Print the title on the gold paper and trim around it. Attach the ribbons, envelopes, title, and medallion to the page.

MATERIALS

- 12" x 12" (30.5 x 30.5 cm) white paper for the background
- 12" x 12" (30.5 x 30.5 cm) blue metal sheet for the background
- white paper
- baseball stickers
- silver metallic photo corners
- silver ribbon border
- colored brads
- preprinted caption box
- computer printer
- blue marker

OPENING DAY

Build it and they will come...to see your embossed sheet metal page.

USE A CIRCLE TEMPLATE and a stylus to draw the circles on the metal sheet. A soft pencil or knitting needle will do the trick. Slightly crinkle the sheet to create texture. (Refer to page 149 for Metal Art.) Attach the sheet to the white paper and draw embossed circles on the sheet. Noting overlaps, arrange and attach the ribbon border, photos, stickers, caption box, and photo corners to the page. Print the titles on the white paper and trim around them. With the tip of a craft knife, pierce a small slit through the title strips, metal sheet, and backing paper. Secure the titles with the brads. Use the marker to complete the caption.

entertaining
spontaneous
energetic
generous
clever

Who could ask for better sisters?

I will go celebrate and sing and laugh.

Sarah, Katie & Jenny

MATERIALS

- 12" x 12" (30.5 x 30.5 cm) lavender paper for the background
- solid papers: white, ivory, blue, tan, and brown
- print papers: lavender texture and green floral
- three tea bags
- dyes: turquoise, blue, and pink
- border rubber stamps
- brown printing ink
- ribbon photo corners
- preprinted caption boxes
- white pipe cleaners
- computer printer
- colored pencils

TEA FOR THREE

Raise your teacup and drink a toast to sisters.

BEFORE DYEING THE TEA BAGS, carefully open each bag and remove the tea. Refold the bags before dipping them in the dye. Mix the turquoise dye to the desired strength. (Refer to page 144 for Dip-Dyed Paper.) Cut the white paper into narrow strips and dip the centers of the strips in the dye. Blot the strips between sheets of paper to make the color uneven. Let dry. Stamp the borders on the vellum. Let dry and cut them into strips. Cut rectangles from the lavender texture and blue papers. Cut a square from the ivory paper. Noting overlaps, arrange and attach the dyed strips, stamped strips, rectangles, and square to the page. Mix the blue and pink dyes to the desired strengths. Dip the bottoms of the bags in the blue dye and let dry. Dip the bottoms of the bags in the pink dye and let dry. Coat the backs of the tea bags and the strings with spray adhesive, and press them in place on the page. The template for the teacup is found on page 205. Cut the shapes from the designated paper colors, layer them, and attach them to the page. Bend short lengths of the pipe cleaner and glue them to the page with small dots of white craft glue. Print the title on the white paper and trim around it. Attach the photos, photo corners, caption boxes, and title to the page. Use the colored pencils to color the title strip and to add additional captions.

MATERIALS

- 12" x 12" (30.5 x 30.5 cm) lavender floral paper for the background
- white paper
- assorted paper scraps of coordinating prints and colors
- vellum: pink and blue print
- fabric swatch
- orange-stitched ribbon
- copper slide frame
- preprinted Mylar caption strip
- bird die cut
- computer printer
- colored pencils

The tang of an apple
the zing in the air
the crunch of the leaves

Autumn is the hush before winter

CRISP AIR OF AUTUMN

Harvest your favorite paper scraps and preserve them with rows of machine stitches.

WHEN MAKING ROWS of machine stitching it is not necessary to mark the paper. Random rows usually look best. Cut small and large sections from the vellum and print papers. Arrange them on the page with the bird die cut and machine stitch over the surface of the layered papers to secure them to the page. Place the photos on the page and slide short lengths of the ribbon under a selected photo. Also tear some edges of the stitched papers away to overlap the photo edges. Attach the ribbons and photos to the page. Print the title on the white paper, trim around it, and color it with the colored pencils. Arrange and attach the fabric swatch, slide frame, caption strip, and title to the page.

NAN

MATERIALS

- 12" x 12" (30.5 x 30.5 cm) green paper for the background
- text print paper
- paper doll wrapping paper
- fabric swatches
- blue ricrac
- assorted paper stars
- stickers: taxi and alphabet
- peach dimensional paint
- rug gripper
- yellow zipper
- cloth or plastic measuring tape
- black colored pencil

At home in her new loft

THE SIMPLE LIFE

Recycle cloth swatches, a zipper, and measuring tape to make a statement that is truly personal.

FOR OBVIOUS REASONS, use new rug gripper for the lace border. Tear wide strips from the text paper. Noting overlaps, arrange and attach the paper and the photos to the page. From the wrapping paper, cut doll silhouette shapes and clothing with irregular border shapes. (Refer to page 150 for Recycled Art.) Cut the fabric swatches and ricrac to match the clothing and coat the backs of the fabric shapes with spray adhesive. Press the fabric in place on the clothing. Cut

the end from the zipper and cut the measuring tape into short strips. Arrange and attach the stars, dolls, clothing, zipper, and measuring tape to the page. Press the stickers in place. Cut a notched corner from the rug gripper. Place it on the corner of the page and squirt dimensional paint in each recess. Let dry. The paint will shrink after drying. Use the pencil to write the caption.

MATERIALS

- 12" x 12" (30.5 x 30.5 cm) light blue paper for the background
- solid papers: white, black, and mint
- pink print paper
- white tracing paper
- pink vellum
- watercolor paints: green, blue, and pink
- pink tulle
- monogram stickers
- rubber cement
- silver leaf paper
- computer printer

PASTEL WAVES

Photo and stickers seem to float on a watery weave of painted vellum.

THERE IS NO RIGHT or wrong way to paint the watercolor on the tracing paper, so just dip in your brush and go with the flow. Paint free-form designs on the tracing paper with the watercolors. Let dry. Tear sections from the tracing paper. Cut wavy strips in the remaining sections and weave them together along with pink vellum strips. (Refer to page 143 for Weaving.) Cut wide strips from the tulle and tear sections from the mint paper. Noting overlaps, arrange and attach the mint paper, painted and woven tracing paper, tulle, and photo on the page. Coat the fronts of the stickers with rubber cement. (Refer to page 18 for Silver Leafing.) Coat the back of the silver leaf film with the rubber cement. After both are dry to the touch, place the film right side up on the stickers and rub. Carefully remove the film. Use the computer printer and the white paper to make the title and tear it into horizontal strips. Paint the strips with the blue watercolor paper and let dry. Cut narrow strips from the black paper and tear a strip from the pink print paper. Arrange and attach the strips, stickers, and title to the page. Use a sewing machine to add stitching in selected areas.

CIRQUE DU SCRAPS

Use contour shapes to make your paper piecing sleek and graceful.

PAY ATTENTION TO THE NOVELTY papers you choose. They add the zing to the page. Trim the pink print, polka dot, and pink vellum papers and attach them to the page. Tear a border strip from the blue paper and trim the blue vellum and novelty papers. Attach them to the page. The templates for the acrobats are found on page 205. (Refer to page 142 for Paper Piecing.) From the melon and white papers, cut mirror images of the torso/legs shape. From the ivory paper, cut mirror images of the head/shoulders shape. From the black and brown papers, cut mirror images of the hair shape. From the pink paper cut one circle 1⅜" (3.5 cm) in diameter. Noting overlaps, arrange and attach the acrobat shapes to the page. Thread assorted paper tags on the ribbon. Arrange and attach the photo, tags, and remaining novelty and print papers to the page. Rub the letters in the page and use the colored pencil to write the text.

MATERIALS

- 12" x 12" (30.5 x 30.5 cm) white paper for the background
- solid papers for the paper pieced acrobats: white, ivory, pink, melon, black, and brown
- blue paper
- pink print paper
- white polka dot paper
- assorted paper scraps of coordinating prints and colors
- assorted scraps of novelty papers
- vellum: pink and blue
- alphabet rub-ons
- blue satin ribbon
- print paper tags
- Eiffel tower die cut
- black colored pencil

MATERIALS

- 12" x 12" (30.5 x 30.5 cm) melon paper for the background
- lemon print paper
- assorted paper scraps of coordinating prints and colors
- acrylic paint: lavender, green, and black
- fine-gauge silver wire
- picture hangers (toothed plates that are attached to the backs of pictures)
- colored eyelets
- mini buckles
- felt scraps: periwinkle and yellow
- lavender paper curling ribbon
- die-cut flowers
- wire captions
- foam adhesive spacers
- black fine-point marker

BEST DRESS

Display wedding finery with cobbled hardware hangers.

THESE CLOSE-UPS are a great way to prove that there was a time when you actually did fit into those clothes. Cut strips from the felt and paper ribbon and stitch or glue the buckles to the strips. (Refer to page 151 for Hardware Accents.) Trim the paper scraps to the desired shapes and attach the scraps, buckle strips, die-cut flowers, and wire captions to the page. Paint the picture hangers with the lavender and green paints and let dry. Secure the hangers to the page with the eyelets. Cut lengths from the wire and loop them around the hangers. Cut rectangles with irregular edges from the lemon paper and mount the photos on the rectangles. Attach them to the page with the foam spacers and tuck the wire ends under the mounted photos. Use the black paint to add the title and let dry.

MATERIALS

- 12" x 12" (30.5 x 30.5 cm) papers: lavender and purple print for the background
- papers for the pieced jesters: blue, ivory fleck and multiprint
- solid papers: green and white
- print papers: gold, blue polka dot, and pink stripe
- paper tags
- metallic ribbon
- assorted alphabet stickers
- preprinted Mylar title strip
- blue brad
- vintage toy stamps
- black printing ink
- colored pencils
- green buttons
- black fine-point marker

IT'S PARTY TIME

Concentric paper circles suggest that on your birthday, the world really does revolve around you.

As an alternative, try making the paper jesters from the wrapping paper or cards left over from the party. Cut large concentric circles in the purple print, gold print, and blue polka dot papers. Arrange them on the page with contrasting papers placed in the gaps behind the circle. Attach the papers to the page. The templates for the jesters are found on page 206. (Refer to page 142 for Paper Piecing.) Cut the head/body shapes from the blue paper and cut the collars from the ivory fleck paper. Cut the remaining shapes from the desired colors.

Cut lengths from the ribbon and attach paper tags to the ends. Cut a triangle from the blue paper to highlight the clear title strip. Noting overlaps, arrange and attach the triangle, jesters, and paper tags to the page. Attach the clear title strip with the brad. Stamp the toys on the white paper and let them dry. Color the shapes with the colored pencils and cut around the shapes. Press the alphabet stickers in place and attach the stamped toys and buttons to the page. Use the marker to draw the faces on the jesters.

MATERIALS

- 12" x 12" (30.5 x 30.5 cm) lavender paper for the background
- pink print vellum
- pink print paper
- assorted paper scraps of coordinating prints and colors
- preprinted title phrases
- alphabet rubber stamps
- printing ink: black and purple
- eyelets: pink and magenta
- silk ribbon: light green, olive, and pink
- die cuts: nosegay and cupcakes
- paper mat
- button
- blue marker

A MOTHER'S SPIRIT

Mother and daughter are tied together with silk ribbon heartstrings.

NOTHING BEATS THE FEEL and drape of silk ribbon. If it is not available at your scrapbook store, you can find it at a needlework store. Cut the desired shapes from the scrap papers and attach them to the page. Cut a strip from the pink print paper and cut a larger strip from the pink vellum. Layer them and attach them to the page. Insert four vertical rows of eyelets on the rectangles. (Refer to page 147 for Stitched Paper.) Thread the silk ribbons through the eyelets and tape the ends to the back of the page to secure. Tie bows in each set of laced ribbons. Cut a length of pink silk ribbon, fold it to form two loops, and attach it to the page. Cut around the title phrase. Noting overlaps, arrange and attach the die-cut flower, paper mat, photos, and remaining paper strips to the page. Also attach the button and die-cut cupcakes to the page. Use the marker, rubber stamps, and ink to complete the title. Cut strips from the scrap papers and fold them around three corners of the page. Secure them on the back with tape.

MATERIALS

- 12" x 12" (30.5 x 30.5 cm) periwinkle paper for the background
- preprinted title box
- print papers: lavender and pink
- novelty hot air balloon papers
- toilet tissue
- liquid starch
- black fine-point marker

L.A. and San Diego —
Venice Beach —
Grauman's Theatre —

HIGH-FLYING VACATION

Yes, these clouds really are made from toilet paper. And, yes, it also comes in pastel colors.

BECAUSE IT REQUIRES several hours to dry, make the faux paper ahead of time. Place a strip of toilet tissue on a plastic sheet and drizzle liquid starch on the tissue. (Refer to page 145 for Faux Handmade Paper.) Pinch and crease at selected areas to create texture and let dry. Using the print papers, novelty paper, and bits of faux handmade paper, piece together two narrow 12" (30.5 cm) strips. Tear the faux paper into cloud shapes and cut a balloon silhouette shape. Noting overlaps, arrange and attach the title box, faux paper clouds, balloon, photos, and pieced strips to the page. Use the marker to write the caption.

MATERIALS

- 12" x 12" (30.5 x 30.5 cm) blue print paper for the background
- solid papers: blue and white
- white print vellum
- watercolor paints: blue, gold, and orange
- preprinted caption box
- alphabet stamps
- black printing ink
- preprinted Mylar caption strip
- narrow strips of novelty papers
- stickers: flower, butterfly, and pressed flowers
- tin tile
- copper mesh
- black fine-point marker

SCHOOL DAYS

Metal works its magic for a school photo touch up.

MAKE SEVERAL REDUCED COPIES of the face on the white paper and have fun painting different versions. Then choose the ones that you like the best. With the black ink, stamp the title on a vellum rectangle. Make two enlarged copies on a commercial copy machine. Also make reduced copies of the photo on the copy machine. Trim the reduced copies as desired and paint them with the watercolor paints. Cut an irregular shape from the blue paper and attach it to the page. Noting overlaps, arrange and attach the photo, photocopies, stamped title, caption strip, and caption box to the page. Press the stickers in place. Cut a rectangle from the copper mesh and fold it over a paper strip. (Refer to page 149 for Metal Art.) Cut photo corners from the tin tile and attach the paper strips and photo corners to the page. Use the marker to write an additional caption.

MATERIALS

- 12" x 12" (30.5 x 30.5 cm) papers: brown print and taupe for the background
- brown mottle paper
- green paper
- assorted paper scraps of coordinating colors
- rubber stamps: alphabet and script
- printing inks: blue and purple
- rub-on caption
- adhesive back metal strips
- brass hinges
- picture hanging tabs (round tabs that attach to the backs of pictures)
- copper wire
- colored brads
- acrylic paint: peach and green
- black colored pencil

DESTINATION HAPPILY EVER AFTER

Hardware done easy: Buy metal accoutrements that have adhesive on the back or attach them with brads and prongs.

THE SHINY FINISH of hinges and rings serves as an interesting contrast to flat paper backgrounds. Tear a section from the brown print paper to reveal the white backing. Cut a section from the brown mottle paper. Cut a window in the section. Arrange and attach the papers and the photos to the page and trim the overlapping edges. Paint the metal strips with the acrylic paints, let them dry, and press them in place. Daub purple printing ink on the hinges and let them dry. Slide paper strips under the edge of one hinge and attach them to the page with the brads. Make the title with the rub-on and alphabet stamps. Using the blue ink, stamp the script on the green paper. The template for the notched shape is found on page 206. Cut out the shape and fold it along the notched edge. Attach the shape to the page with the tabs. (Refer to page 151 for Hardware Accents.) Thread the copper wire through one tab and unravel the ends. Use the colored pencil to write the caption.

MATERIALS

- 12" x 12" (30.5 x 30.5 cm) papers: pink print and white for the background
- bronze paper
- white tissue paper
- assorted paper scraps of coordinating prints and colors
- rub-on title
- preprinted clear caption box
- white scallop border
- white acrylic paint
- air-drying modeling clay
- black colored pencil

BEACH BABIES

Stir up a batch of light-as-air sand dollars to spice up your page.

MAKE THE SAND DOLLARS ahead of time because they require several days of drying time. Dilute white acrylic paint and apply a thin wash over selected black-and-white photos. Cut circles from the air-drying modeling clay for the sand dollars. Press the end of a pencil in the soft clay to make the center designs. (Refer to page 146 for Clay Art.) After the clay has dried, sand the edges at an angle. Cut silhouettes of a couple from the bronze paper. Tear the center from the pink print paper and cut circle shapes around the outside edges. Noting overlaps, arrange and attach the pink print paper, photos, trimmed paper, and assorted scraps to the page. Rub the title over a paper scrap and attach the clear caption box. Attach the scallop border and sand dollars to the page. Tear shapes from the tissue paper and coat the backs with adhesive spray. Press them in place on the page and trim the overlapping edges. Use the pencil to write an additional caption.

MATERIALS

- 12" x 12" (30.5 x 30.5 cm) turquoise embossed paper for the background
- solid papers: blue and white
- die-cut letters
- plastic film
- acrylic paint: yellow, orange, and red
- computer printer

fall fall fall fall
fall our favorite
time of the year
fall fall fall fall
fall fall fall fall
fall fall fall fall
fall fall fall fall

OUR FAVORITE TIME OF THE YEAR

Set your page ablaze with fiery fluttering leaves.

WHEN CREATING THE PAINTED LEAVES, there may be some areas that don't peel uniformly as you lift the leaves. Like everything in nature, these irregularities will make your prints unique. Cut sections from the blue paper and attach them to the page. Place the leaves right side up on a sheet of scrap paper and paint the leaves. (Refer to page 148 for Film Overlay.) Let the paint dry and coat the backs of the leaves with spray adhesive. Arrange the leaves as desired and press them in place on a second sheet of scrap paper. Cut sections from the film and remove the backing paper. Cover the leaves with the film and, using your finger as a brayer, rub the film that is directly over the painted surfaces. Slowly peel the film from the leaves to lift the paint. Press the painted film sections in place on the page and trim the overlapping edges. Print the title on the white paper and trim around the edges. Attach the photos, die-cut letters, and title box to the page.

MATERIALS

- 12" x 12" (30.5 x 30.5 cm) cream speckled paper for the background
- solid papers: white, blue, and gold
- print papers: lavender and metallic floral
- toilet tissue
- white craft glue
- dried lavender
- print tissue
- paper flower petals
- wrapped floss dolls
- paisley rubber stamps
- purple printing ink
- watercolor paints: pink and green
- assorted paper scraps of coordinating prints and colors
- plastic film
- computer printer

Everybody knows that *angels* come in all shapes and sizes.

This one is three feet tall and she likes pizza.

YOUNG ANGEL

This combination of photo and border is truly heaven sent.

MAKE THE FAUX PAPER with embedded stems ahead of time because the paper requires several hours to dry. Arrange the lavender stems on a sheet of plastic and place a strip of toilet tissue over the stem tops. Mix white craft glue with water. (Refer to page 145 for Faux Handmade Paper.) Evenly cover the tissue with the diluted glue and let dry. Stamp the paisley shapes on the blue paper, let them dry, and trim around the shapes. Trim the print papers and gold paper to the desired sizes and attach the stamped shapes and trimmed papers to the page. Tear around the lavender stems. Noting overlaps, arrange and attach the faux paper and stems, tissue paper, wrapped dolls, and paper petals to the page. Print the title on the white paper and cut around the phrases. Paint them with the watercolor paint and let dry. Attach the photo and the title strips to the page.

TEMPLATES

All templates are actual size. Resize them on a commercial copier if your compositions require shapes that are larger or smaller than the sizes provided.

First, transfer the template by using a pencil to trace it onto tracing paper. Be as accurate as possible, especially for templates that are complex or small in scale. When paper piecing (see page 142), some shapes will overlap others, so allow excess paper along the edges that will be covered by adjoining shapes. Next, carefully cut the tracing paper along the marked lines. Then, hold the pattern firmly in place on the paper while drawing around the cut edge. Trace pieces that are to be cut from the same paper (such as rabbits or butterflies) in groups, allowing ¼" (6 mm) between the pieces.

If you choose to draw the shape on the wrong side of the paper, turn it wrong-side-up before tracing. Use an air-soluble marking pen to transfer shapes to fabric. The ink from an air-soluble marker will disappear in 48 to 72 hours. It can also be removed by rinsing with cold water. Look for one at your local fabric store.

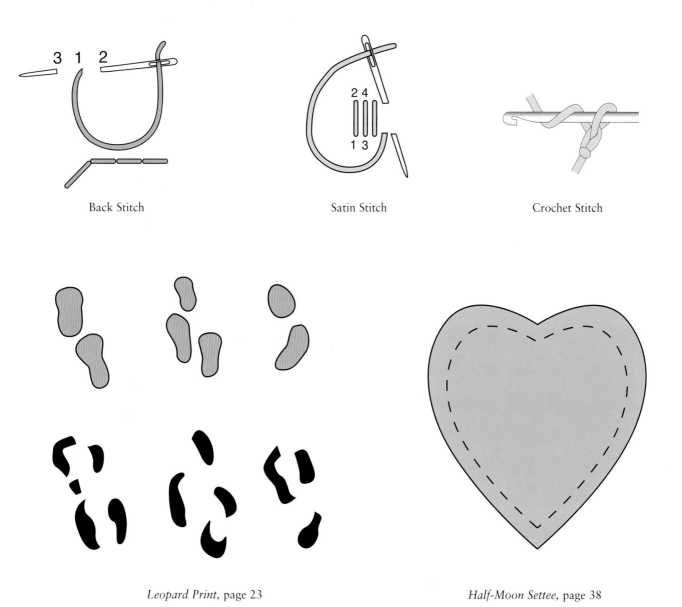

Back Stitch

Satin Stitch

Crochet Stitch

Leopard Print, page 23

Half-Moon Settee, page 38

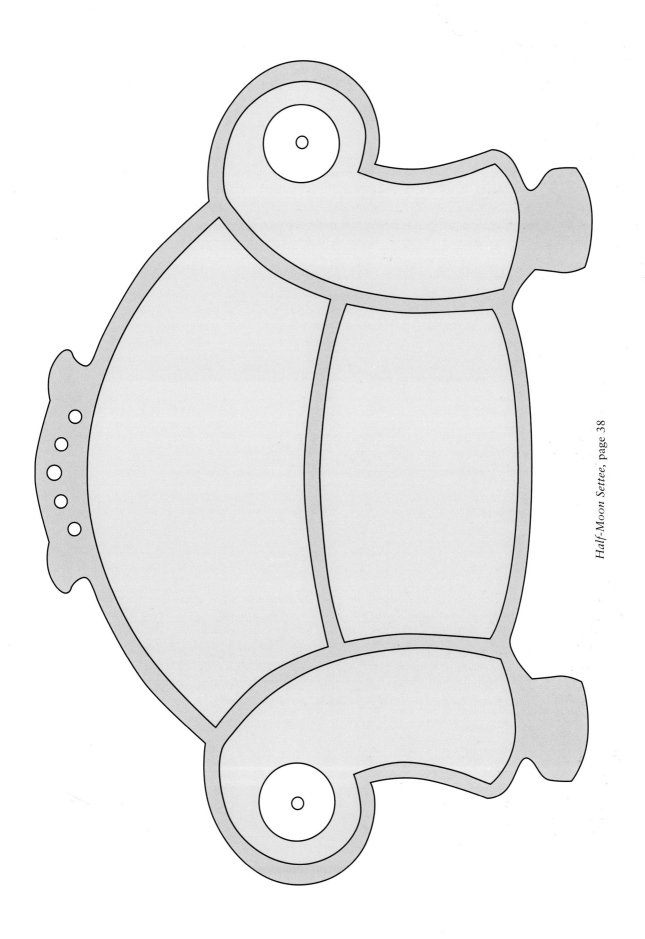

Half-Moon Settee, page 38

College Graduation, 1897, page 40

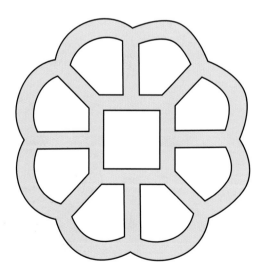

Surprise Package, page 43

Flower Girl and Fretwork
(small corner), page 45

Flower Girl and Fretwork
(large corner), page 45

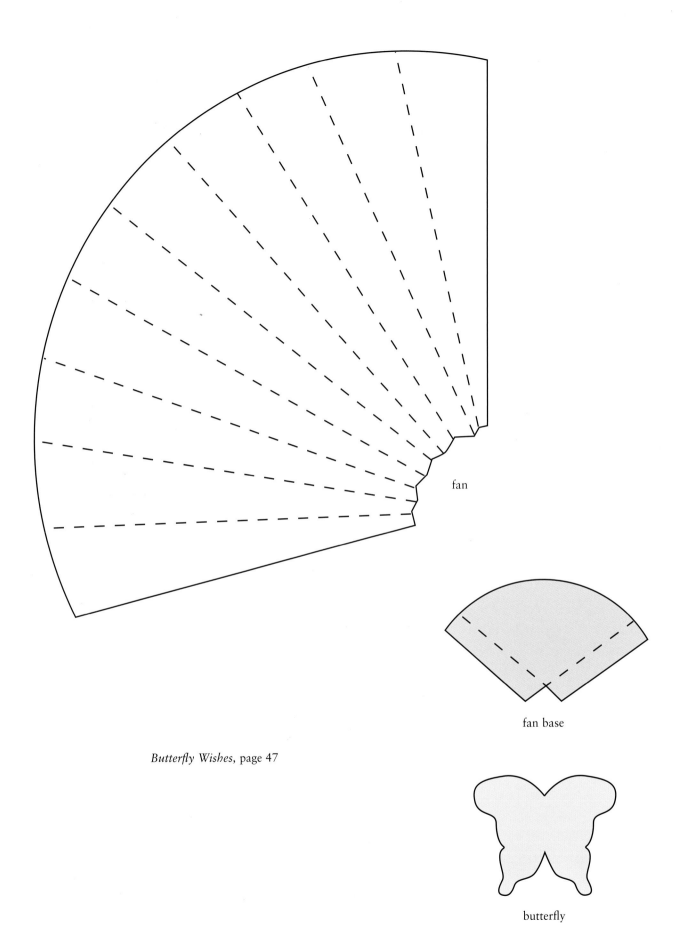

fan

fan base

Butterfly Wishes, page 47

butterfly

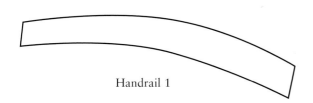

Handrail 1

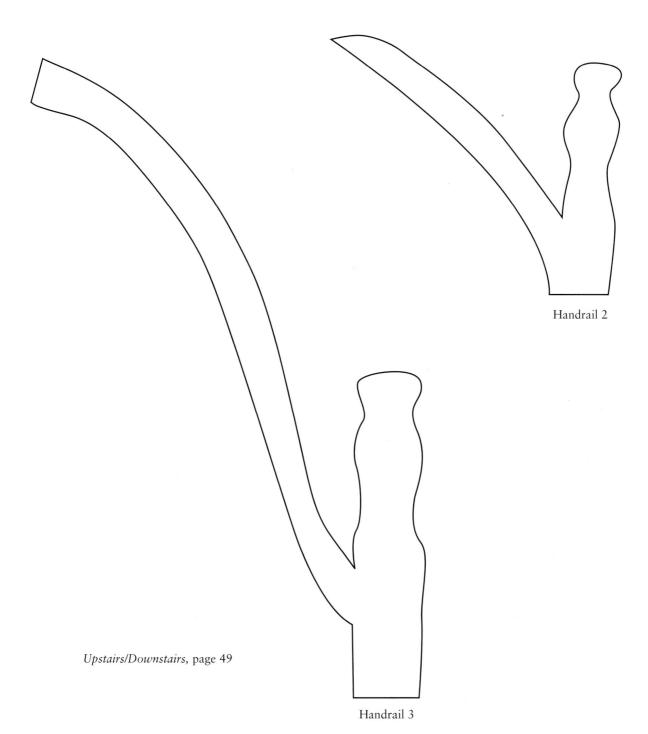

Handrail 2

Upstairs/Downstairs, page 49

Handrail 3

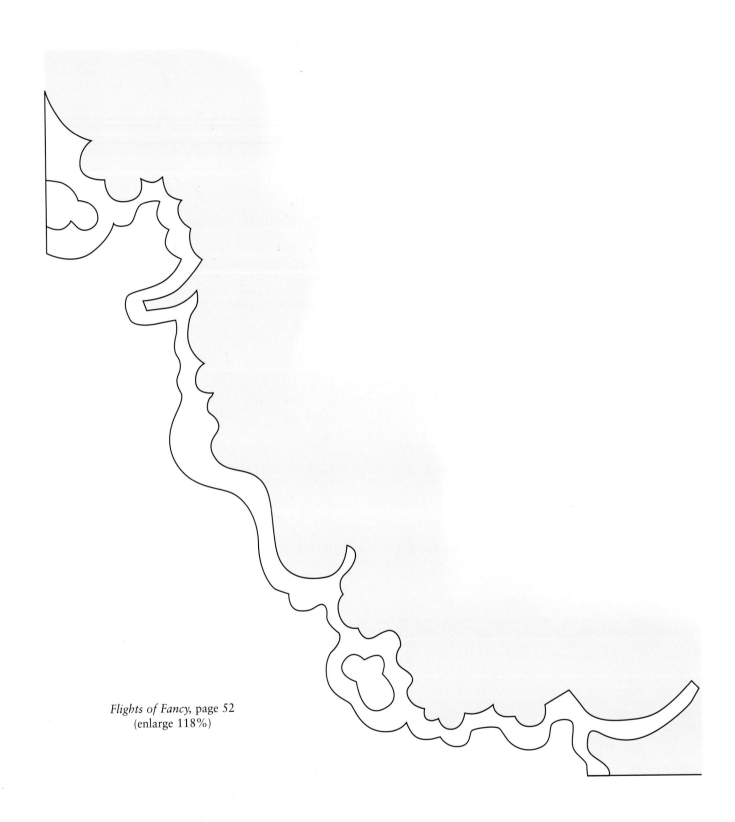

Flights of Fancy, page 52
(enlarge 118%)

The Immigrant Song, page 54

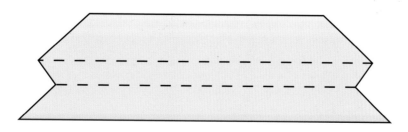

A Gentle Age, page 56

Baby's Day Out, page 62

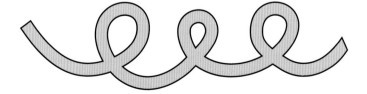

Long Ago and Not So Far Away, page 63

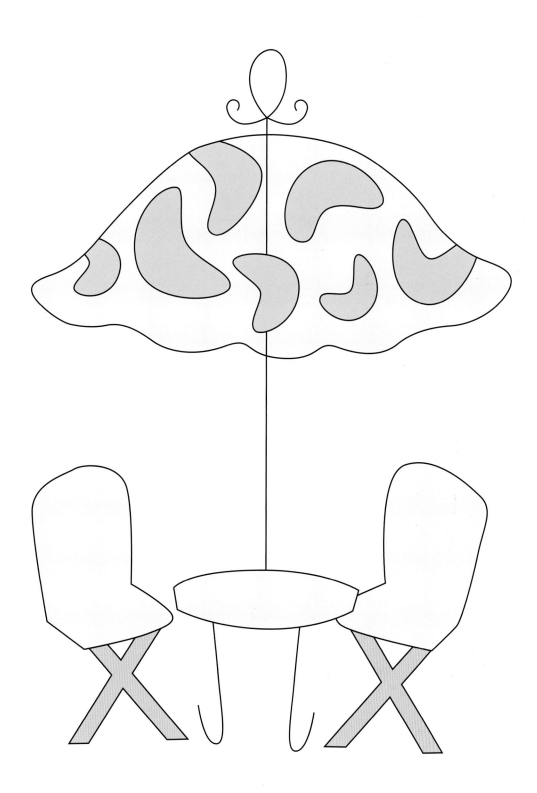

Pool Party, page 78

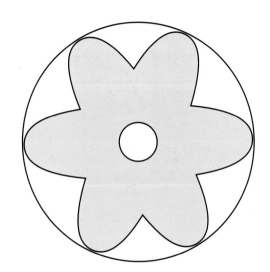

Blush, page 79

A List of Rhymes, page 81

The Best Things in Life, page 80

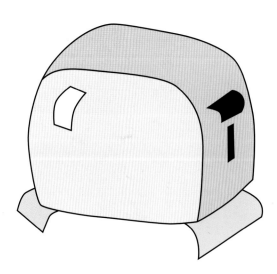

Toast and Jam, page 84

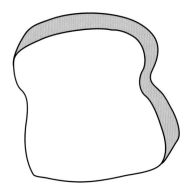

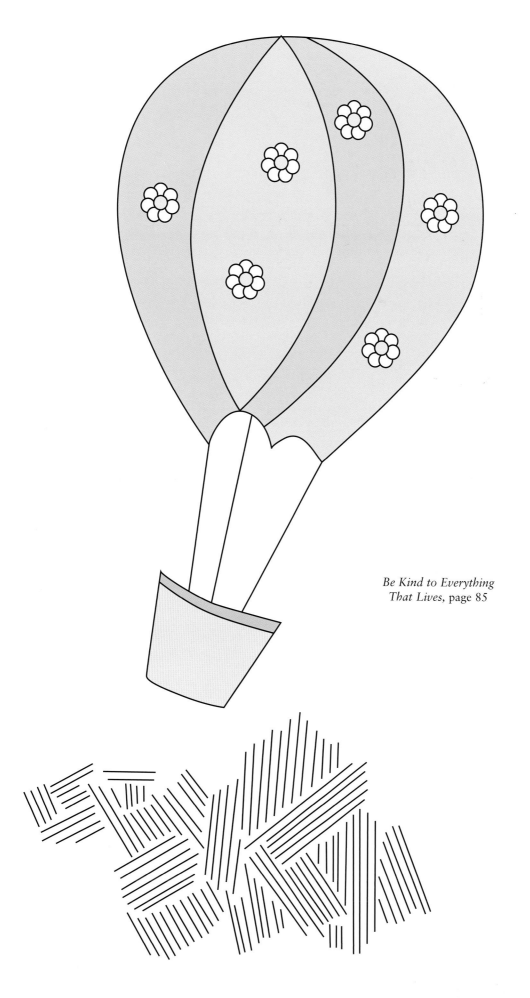

Be Kind to Everything That Lives, page 85

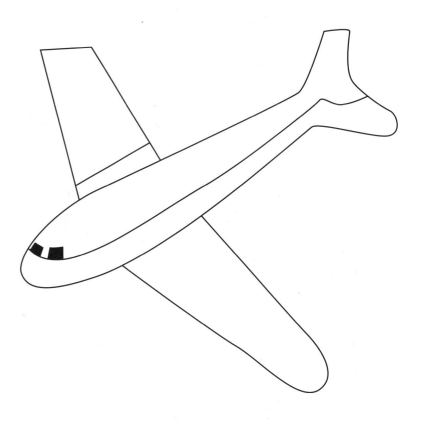

Which Way to the Beach? page 86

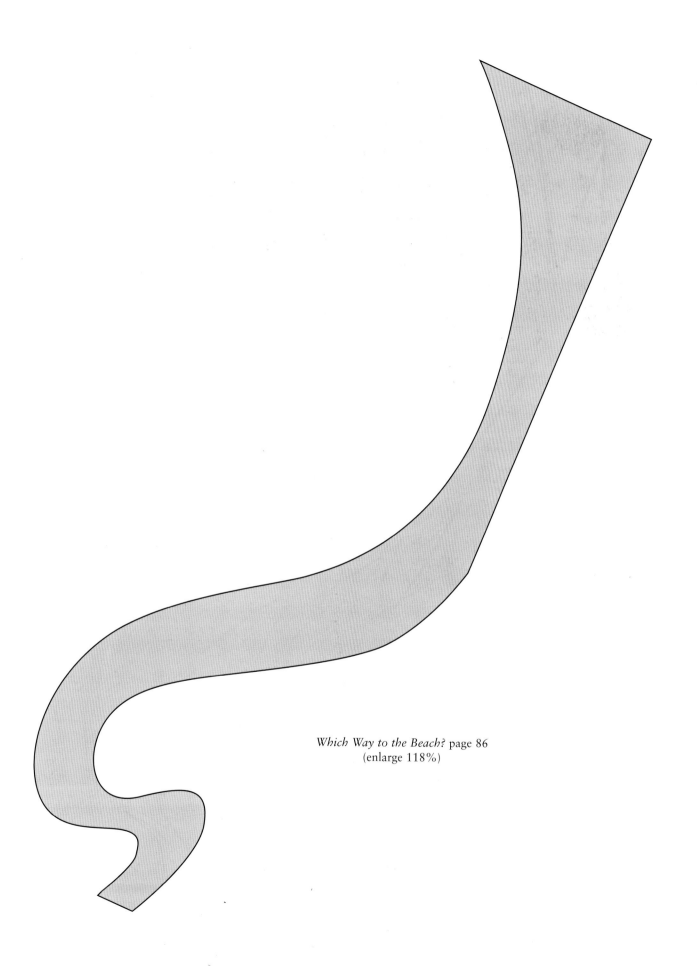

Which Way to the Beach? page 86
(enlarge 118%)

Blue Hawaii,
page 102

Love the Earth, page 105

Guardian Angel, page 107

Guardian Angel, page 107

FRIENDS

American Graffiti, page 109

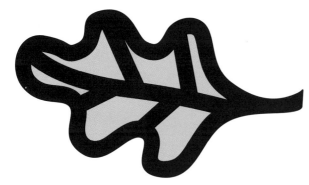

Leaf 1

Leaf 2

Leaf 3

Higher Education, page 126

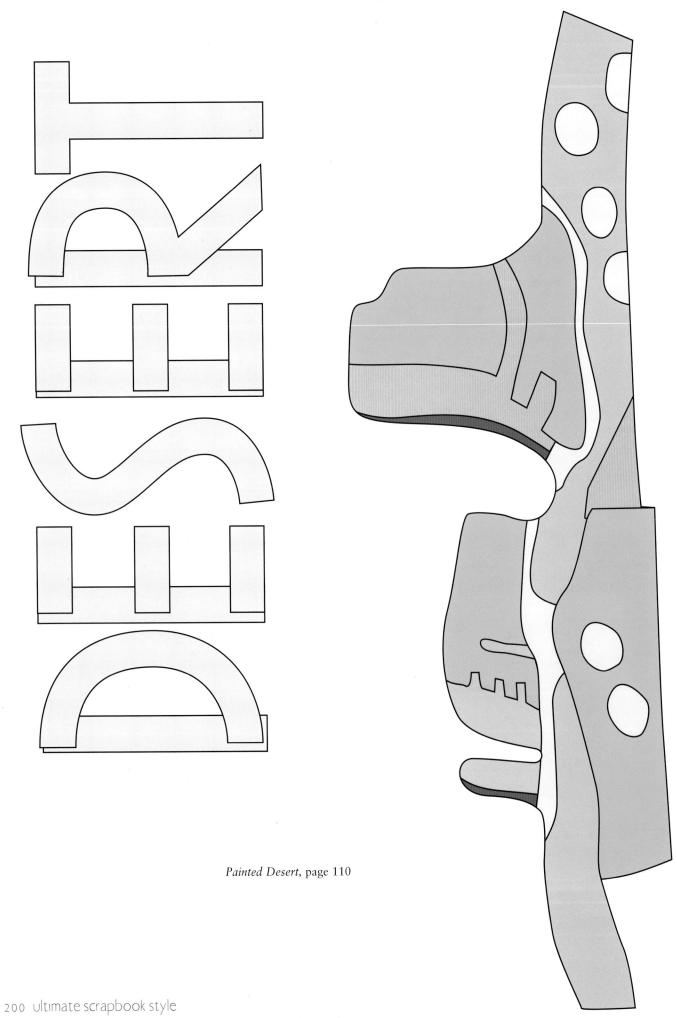

Painted Desert, page 110

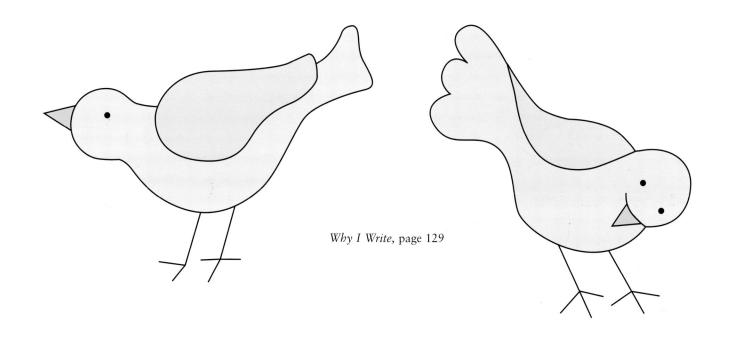

Why I Write, page 129

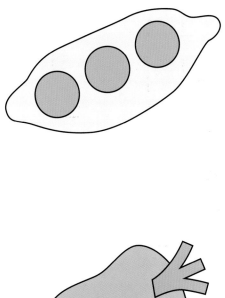

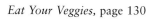

Eat Your Veggies, page 130

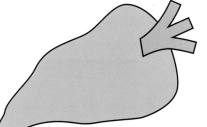

Book Talk, page 135

Road Trip, page 136

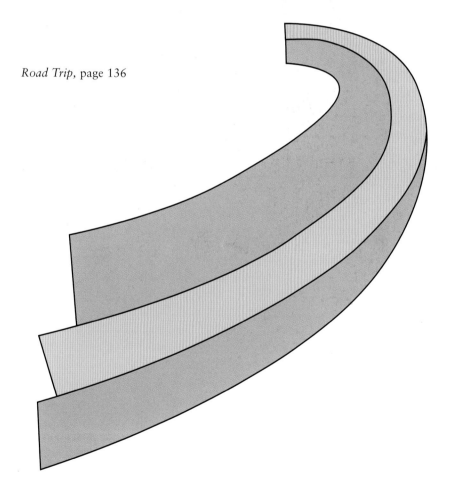

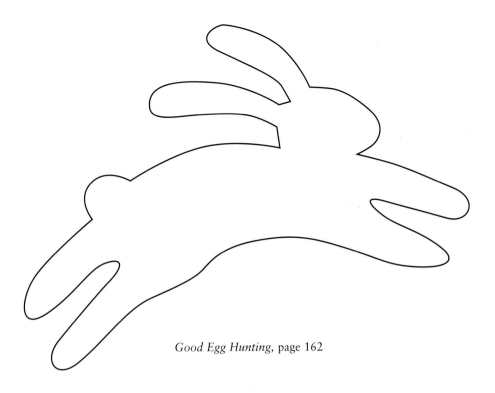

Good Egg Hunting, page 162

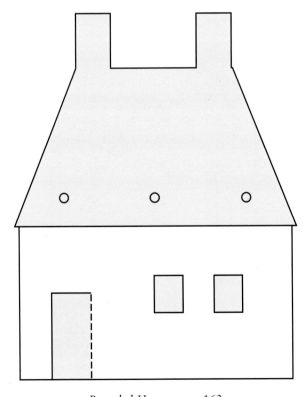

Recycled House, page 163

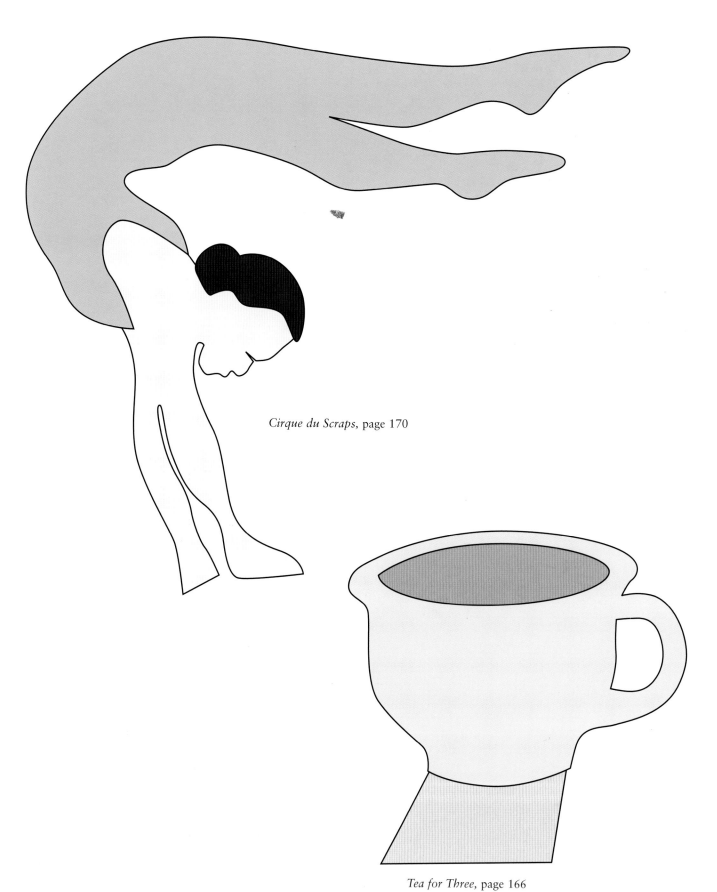

Cirque du Scraps, page 170

Tea for Three, page 166

It's Party Time, page 172

Destination Happily Ever After, page 176

RESOURCES

3M
www.mmm.com
spray adhesive

ACTIVA
www.activaproducts.com
colored sand

AITOH ORIGAMI
www.dickblick.com
origami paper

AMERICAN ART CLAY
www.amaco.com
polymer clay

AMERICAN CRAFT
www.americancraft.com
paper

ARTISTIC WIRE
www.artisticwire.com
wire

AUSSIE SCRAPBOOK
SUPPLIERS
www.scrapbooking.about.com
supplies (Australia)

BERWICK OFFRAY LLC.
www.berwickindustries.com
ribbon

BLICK ART MATERIALS
www.dickblick.com
macramé supplies

CANADIAN SCRAPBOOK
STORES
www.welovescrapbooking.com
supplies (Canada)

CANSON
www.canson-us.com
paper

CHATTERBOX
www.chatterboxinc.com
letter stencils

CLEARSNAP, INC.
www.clearsnap.com
ink pads

CRAYOLA
www.crayola.com
crayons

CREATIVE PAPER CLAY
www.paperclay.com
air-drying modeling clay

DAISY D'S PAPER
www.daisydspaper.com
paper

DARICE
www.darice.com
craft foam

DIE CUTS WITH A VIEW
www.diecutswithaview.com
ribbon, embellishments

DMC
www.dmc-usa.com
embroidery floss

DMD INDUSTRIES
www.dmdind.com
paper, tissue paper

DOVER PUBLICATIONS
www.doverpublications.com
decorative papers

DUNCAN ENTERPRISES
www.duncancrafts.com
3-D paint, dye

EK SUCCESS
www.eksuccess.com
pens, markers

ELMER'S GLUE
www.elmers.com
white craft glue

FISKARS
www.fiskars.com
scissors

FRAMCA XENIA
www.paperworld.co.za
supplies (South Africa)

GLITTEREX CORP.
908-272-9121
glitter (USA)

THE GOLD LEAF COMPANY
www.goldleafcompany.com
composition gold leaf

GRAFIX
www.grafixarts.com
shrink plastic

HALCRAFT
www.halcraft.com
beads

HANDMADE-PAPER
www.handmade-paper.us
mulberry paper

HERO ARTS
www.heroarts.com
rubber stamps

HIRSCHBERG SCHUTZ & CO.
908-810-1111
decorative trim (USA)

INTERNATIONAL
SCRAPBOOK STORES
www.memorymakers.com/
locator/store
supplies (international)

JHB INTERNATIONAL
www.buttons.com
buttons

KAREN FOSTER DESIGN
www.karenfosterdesign.com
paper

LAKE CITY CRAFT CO.
www.quilling.com
quilling supplies

LAMPLIGHT FEATHER
www.tonyhill.net
feathers

LASTING IMPRESSIONS
www.lastingimpressions.com
ribbon

LIL DAVIS
www.lildavisdesigns.com
paper, trinkets

LIPTON
www.lipton.com
tea

MAKING MEMORIES
www.makingmemories.com
metal keys

MAMELOK PRESS
www.mamelok.com
découpage paper

MY MIND'S EYE
www.mymindseye.com
paper frames, preprinted titles

PALMER
www.palmerpaint.com
poster paint

PEBBLES INC.
www.pebbles.com
paper

PERSONAL IMPRESSIONS
www.richstamp.co.uk
supplies (United Kingdom)

PLAID ENTERPRISES
www.plaidonline.com
*acrylic paints, silk ribbons,
foam stamps*

POLYFORM PRODUCTS CO.
www.sculpey.com
polymer clay

PRISM
www.prismpapers.com
paper

PSX
www.psxdesign.com
rubber stamps

RANGER INDUSTRIES
www.rangerink.com
ink pads

ROSE ART
www.roseart.com
fuzzy posters, markers

RUBBER STAMPEDE, INC.
www.rubberstampede.com
rubber stamps

RUSTY PICKLE
www.rustypickle.com
paper, rub-ons, tags

SANFORD CORPORATION
www.sanfordcorp.com
colored pencils

SEI
www.shopsei.com
paper, trim, brads, mini doilies

STAMPENDOUS
www.stampendous.com
embossing grains

STAMPERIA
www.stamperia.com
supplies (Italy)

STA-FLO
www.purex.com
liquid starch

STICKER STUDIO
www.stickerstudio.com
stickers

SUNDAY INTERNATIONAL
www.sundayint.com
rubber stamps

THE PAPER COMPANY
www.anwcrestwood.com
quilling paper

THERM O WEB
www.thermoweb.com
double-sided adhesive

TSUKIINEKO
www.tsukineko.com
stamping ink

WESTRIM
www.westrimcrafts.com
wire

WIMPOLE STREET
CREATIONS
www.wimpolestreet.com
gauze, embellishments

XACTO PRODUCTS
www.xactoproducts.com
craft knives

ACKNOWLEDGMENTS

"The capacity to care is the thing that gives life its deepest meaning and significance." —Pablo Casals

Thanks to those of you who take the process of preserving memories seriously. Although making scrapbooks is often regarded as a frivolous pastime, you are creating pages that will amuse and intrigue generations to come. The only thing that future generations may know about you is that you cared enough to preserve the spirit of special occasions and everyday moments. And if this is what they know of you, it will be enough.

Also thanks to Mary Ann Hall and Rochelle Bourgault of Rockport Publishers, and Kevin Dilley and Cherie Hanson.

ABOUT THE AUTHOR

Trice Boerens has worked in the craft industry for the past 22 years as an author, writer, and designer for numerous books and magazines. Although textiles featuring needlework and quilting have been a central focus, she also designs jewelry, greeting cards, children's books, home accessories, and even tattoos. She has also done design work for other companies including the Disney Corporation, Blue Mountain Arts, and the Campbell's Soup Corporation. She is a graduate of Brigham Young University with a degree in art education and graphic design. She is author of several Quarry books, including most recently *Scrapbook Collage: The Art of Layering Translucent Materials* (2005).